Blowing Zen I

GW00857604

Carl Abbott, Santa Cruz, California

A Heads Up!

First!

Please understand the musical scores in this book begin at the back and progresses toward the front of the book. That means *page 1 starts at the end of the book*. This right to left reading is how this Japanese music is written.

This volume carries on where "Blowing Zen" left off. It contains musical scores for additional Hon Kyoku, San Kyoku and Japanese folk music.

Go on line

Downloads MP3 recordings of many of the Hon Kyoku in this book, bonus materials, and other information at: Centertao.org/learn-zen. Also, be sure to revisit the site once in awhile as we will continue to place additional resources there.

Problems?

If you have problems with any of this material, and conscientious attempts to solve them fail, please email me a Centertao.org or write. Enclose a self-addressed stamped envelope and send to: Center For Taoist Thought And Fellowship, 406 Lincoln St., Santa Cruz, CA. 95060

Copy the sheet music

Copy the music so you can read it while referring to the instructions. You can glue the edges of these copies into one long sheet, moving from right to left, and then fold it in an accordion fashion. This will allow you to play the long pieces without having to turn pages.

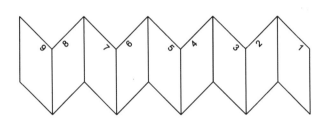

中道
CenterTao.org

TABLE OF CONTENTS

- Page 1 begins at the back of this book -

SHAKUHACHI FINGERING CHART

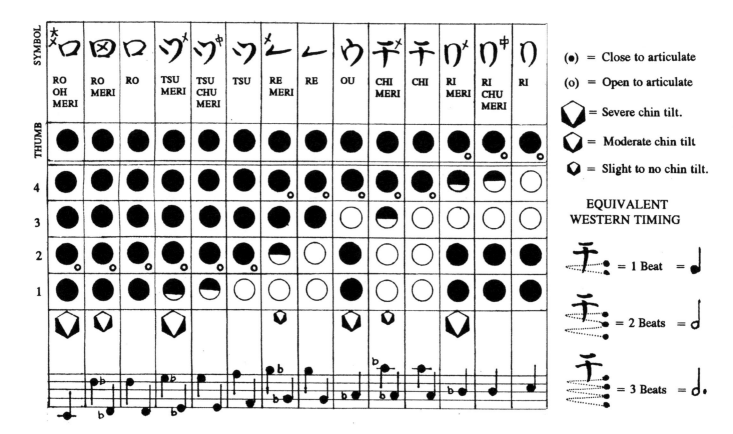

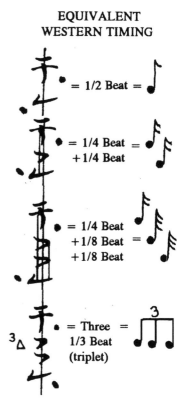

NOTE: The notes from OU SAN thru HA YON GO
are played high octave only, except occasionally in
Buddhist Hon Kyoku.

THE SHEET MUSIC

One inconvenience you'll find in playing the sheet music is that you must interrupt your playing while you turn to the next page of notation. To solve this problem try the following:

Xerox the sheet music. Then glue the first page of notation to the second, and these in turn to the next and so on which will result in a single sheet of notation 20 plus feet. You now fold this long sheet accordion fashion. This allows you to lay open to any length of notation and read and play continuously.

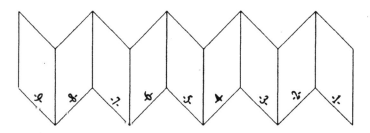

In order to have enough margin to glue on, you must position each page of notation on the copy machine so that you have a wider margin on the left side of each page. Doing a careful job will result in a much better finished product

SAN KYOKU PIECES, Page 1 - 14

It takes a while to find San Kyoku music really pleasurable to play or listen to. After much playing you gradually acquire an aesthetic appreciation for it. For most Westerners it is mostly just noise in the beginning. Even so, it is important to play it awhile because it trains technique and timing. Whether you want to play it long enough to develop a love for it is another matter. Actually the more skilled you become at Hon Kyoku the more you will be able to use the sensitivity learned through it in San Kyoku, which in turn will make it more satisfying to play.

If you have studied "Blowing Zen" conscientiously you should know all you need to for the San Kyoku in this booklet. If you are unsure of some parts, try to improvise. Here and there you will find double columns of notation. Play the right column and if you are playing with someone else, they play the left.

FOLK MUSIC, Page 46 - 54

The folk tunes are nice to play for a change. They have a more recognizable melody which can be more pleasing to western ears. Try playing them at different tempos using side to side sway timing or 1/2 timing.

HON KYOKU PIECES, Page 14 - 23

I have included PITCH GRAPHS for these pieces. The graph for each piece contains only the important sections or phrases of the piece which are new, i.e., the ones you have not encountered yet. Don't take these graphs too literally. They are meant to suggest ways to play: to give you an idea of what is possible. But really there are no hard and fast rules.

HON KYOKU PIECES, Page 24 - 45

After studying the pitch graphs and playing the music for the Hon Kyoku on pages 14 to 23, you should know enough to play these pieces, Once you have a firm understanding of what is involved in Hon Kyoku you can improvise with certainty.

Shika No Tone on page 28 is a duet. If you play alone, play both columns one after the other. Kumoi Jishi on page 29 is a duet for two or three players. The main melody is found on the central column. The right hand column is for the 2nd player, and the left hand column is for a third player who plays a NI SHAKU (60.5 cm. long flute). To obtain the highest benefit and pleasure from Hon Kyoku it is important to keep in mind the Taoist principle of 'actionless action'.

PITCH GRAPHS FOR HON KYOKU
(see top of next page)

(A). Title of the Hon Kyoku piece.

(B). The numbers indicate the column in which the following phrases are located, e.g., 2 would be the second column from the right.

(C). Two measure marks (o's) one below the other show that some notation has been left out between them. Take, for example, the pitch graphs of these 3 unconnected phrases from column 1 of Takiochi No Kyoku.

NOTE: The graph lines don't always coincide with the note graphed. Sometimes these lines are below the note and sometimes above.

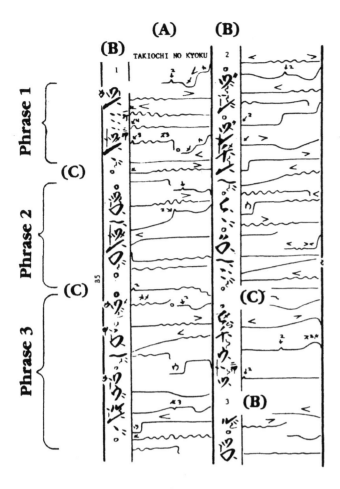

(A) **(B)**

(B) TAKIOCHI NO KYOKU 2

Phrase 1

(C)

Phrase 2

(C) **(C)**

Phrase 3

(B)

POINTS 1 to 58
Notation, pitch graph symbols and phrases.

NOTATION

1. This HA is played with all the fingers off all the holes, and a slight chin tilt. This is also indicated by a dot inside the HA (　　　　)

2. This indicates that you can repeat the preceding phrase or section, starting at the bracket mark (　　　　). You need not do this in the beginning years of playing. It is optional.

3. This is similar to a measure mark. It is a good place to breathe if you have not done so earlier.

4. This grace note is called a 'Keshi'. It should be very subtle.

5. The pitch goes to a deep MERI (OH MERI) and then returns to the pitch you were playing.

6. The pitch goes more KARI (sharper) and then it returns, or it slides to the next note.

7. The pitch first goes to a deep MERI, then goes very KARI, and finally slides to the next note.

8. The pitch rises very gradually and slightly towards the end of the note.

9. You make a RU type articulation by striking hole #1 with the ring finger.

10. RU type articulation on hole #2.

11. RU type articulation on hole #3.

12. ATARI type articulation on hole #2.

13. ATARI type articulation on hole #3.

PITCH GRAPH SYMBOLS
14. ATARI (sometimes without ↓) usually with hole number shown.

15. RU (sometimes without ⅃) usually with hole number shown.

16. MERI

17. OH MERI

18. SURU with hole number usually shown.

19. Quick transition/finer movement.

20. Volume increases.

21. Volume decreases.

22. Tempo increases - play note shorter.

23. Tempo decreases - play note longer.

24. Slight pause for breath.

25. YURI

26. Relative pitch change for the note.

27. KO RO: Play HA but open and close holes #1 and #2 alternately, quickly and smoothly.

28. Slightly but rapidly shake flute toward and then away from lip.

29. Grace note TSU.

30. Grace note OU.

COMMON HON KYOKU PHRASES

The following, #31 to #58, are common phrases used in Hon Kyoku. See their notation on the next page (B4). A selection of these is recorded on the last track of the Blowing Zen CD.

31. Slide gradually from TSU to RE, then slide slightly to RO.

32. Shift abruptly from TSU MERI to TSU and then to RE.

33. Shift from (TSU) MERI to OH MERI, then do an ATARI of RO as you abruptly shift to RO.

34,35. End each RO in RO MERI - two beats for #34 and one beat for #35.

36. TSU is played KARI for the first beat. Then it returns to the usual MERI. It returns to KARI with an articulation on the upbeat. Then it returns to MERI before going to RE.

37. When HI is MERI, CHI is usually KARI.

Squiggly lines that bend left represent MERI shifts. Those that bend right represent KARI shifts. Here it bends both ways - first left into MERI and then right into KARI.

38. When HI is KARI, CHI is usually MERI. CHI is usually MERI in Hon Kyoku even when not indicated. Playing what sounds right works fine.

39. The squiggly line shows that OU bends up to KARI before the ATARI. Play OH KARI by extending your finger off holes #1 and #3, but not off the flute. Also extend the chin out to maximize the KARI. Then shift abruptly back to MERI on the ATARI.

40. The volume of HA diminishes almost to silence just before an abrupt shift to RO.

41. HA goes from MERI to KARI, then after a RU tap on hole #2, goes back to MERI, then back to KARI again.

42. Notice the small KARI symbol placed inside the HA. HA rises abruptly from MERI to KARI just before the right beat mark.

43. Listen to the grace note OU, then HI, then HI MERI, then HI with articulation, then HI MERI again followed by a trill to HI GO.

44. Listen to the volume changes and where the breath is taken.

45. HI GO ATARI's shift to HI ATARI's.

46. Slightly but rapidly shake the flute towards and then away from the lip.

47. Like #46, but shake at the end of OU, as shown by the double line.

48. You can use this, MURA IKI, on most notes. The blast of air and sound occurs on the full KARI of the note. Then it lowers to MERI with a little YURI.

49. The first HA goes slightly KARI before it shifts to high octave. Also notice the increase in tempo.

50. This begins with a low octave grace note OU. Notice the increasing tempo.

51. Play this, KO RO, by playing HA, opening and closing holes #1 and #2 alternately, quickly and smoothly. Notice the grace note HA before OU.

52. This is a KO RO of HA GO and HI MERI. Play HA GO and HI MERI as usual, but open and close holes #1 and #2 alternately like #51. Slide off hole #2 when going to HI MERI.

53. Thumb makes RU type articulation on the back hole.

54. Thumb brushes counter clockwise across hole #5

55. Thumb brushes clockwise across hole #5.

56. The first two OSHI YURIs end in MERI. The remainder are never overly MERI, and end in KARI.

57. Each repeat mark means to repeat CHI and RU. Then play a series of RUs in low octave.

58. Most Hon Kyoku end with this. When playing RE, leave hole #1 closed.

Hon Kyoku symbols and notation.

ロ	RO	
ツ	TSU	
一	RE	
ウ	OU	
千	CHI	
リ	RI	
ハ	HA	
(1)	HA	
ハ	HA (open holes)	
く	HI	
く	HI GO	
カ	RYO	
甲	KAN	
	ATARI + 2 beat marks	
	NAYASHI	
ル	RU	
	YURI	
カ	KARI	
メ	MERI	
(2)	REPEAT PRECEDING PHRASE (optional)	
(3) ○	MEASURE 'marks'	

Pitch graph symbols.

(4)
(5)
(6)
(7)
(8)
(9)
(10)
(11)
(12)
(13)
(14)
(15)
(16)
(17)
(18)
(19)
(20) <
(21) >
(22)
(23)
(24) ○
(25)
(26)
(27)
(28)
(29)
(30)

Examples of some common phrases used in Hon Kyoku which are recorded on Track 27.

(31) (32) (33) (34) (35) (36) (37) (38) (39) (40) (41)
(42) (43) (44) (45) (46) (47) (48)
(49) (50) (51) (52) (53) (54) (55)
(56) (57) (58)

B4

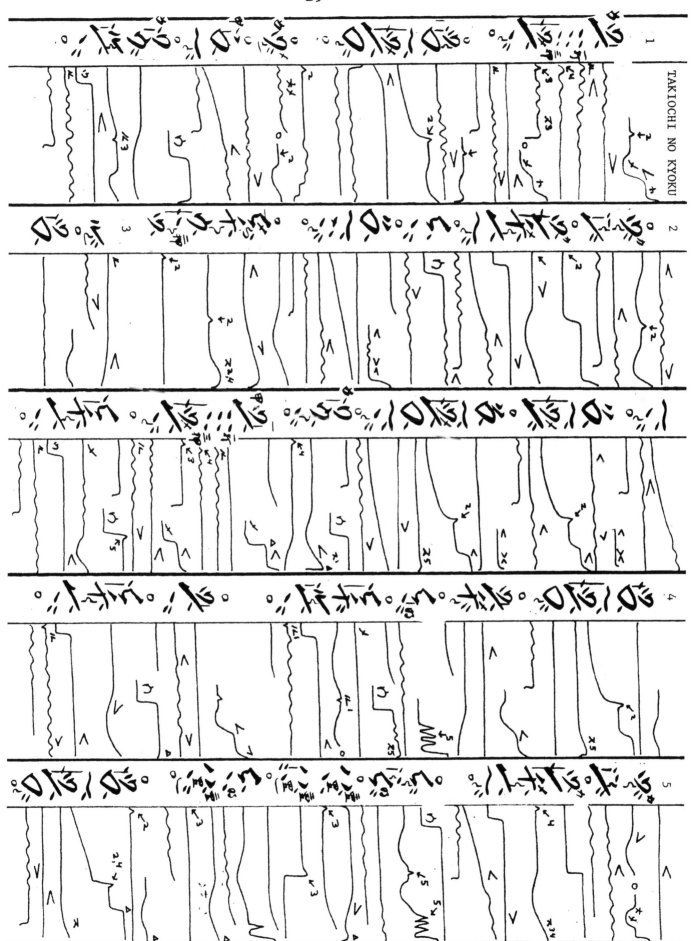

TAKIOCHI NO KYOKU

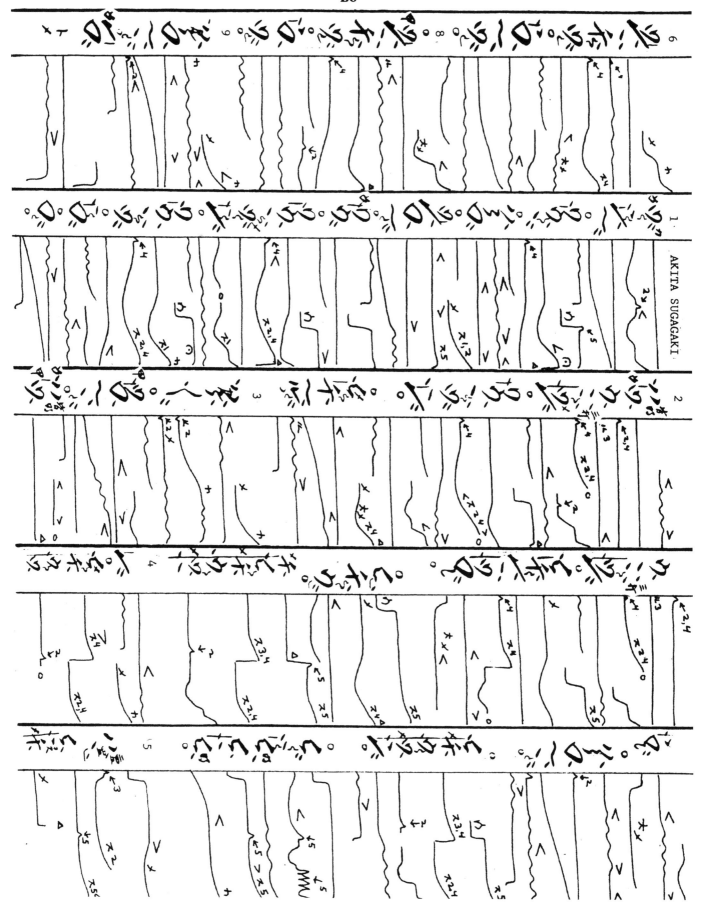

AKITA SUGAGAKI.

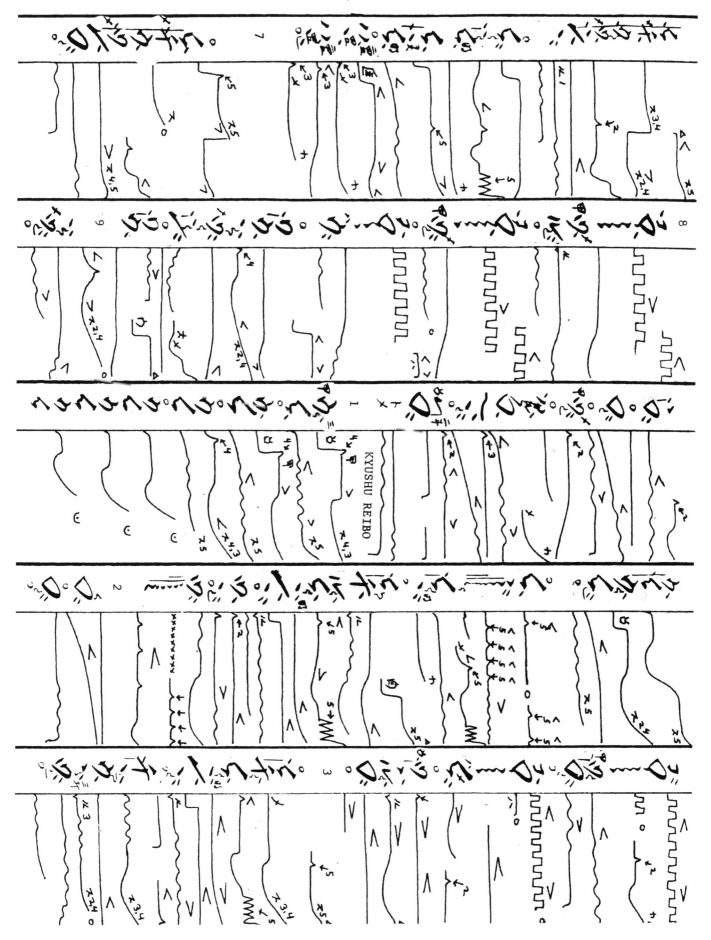

KYUSHU REIBO

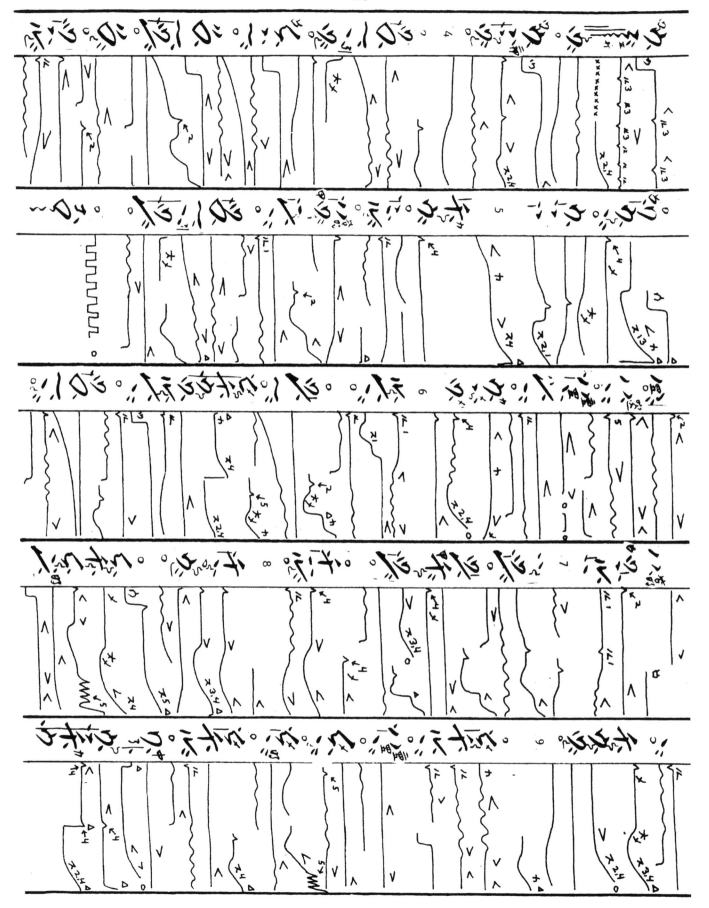

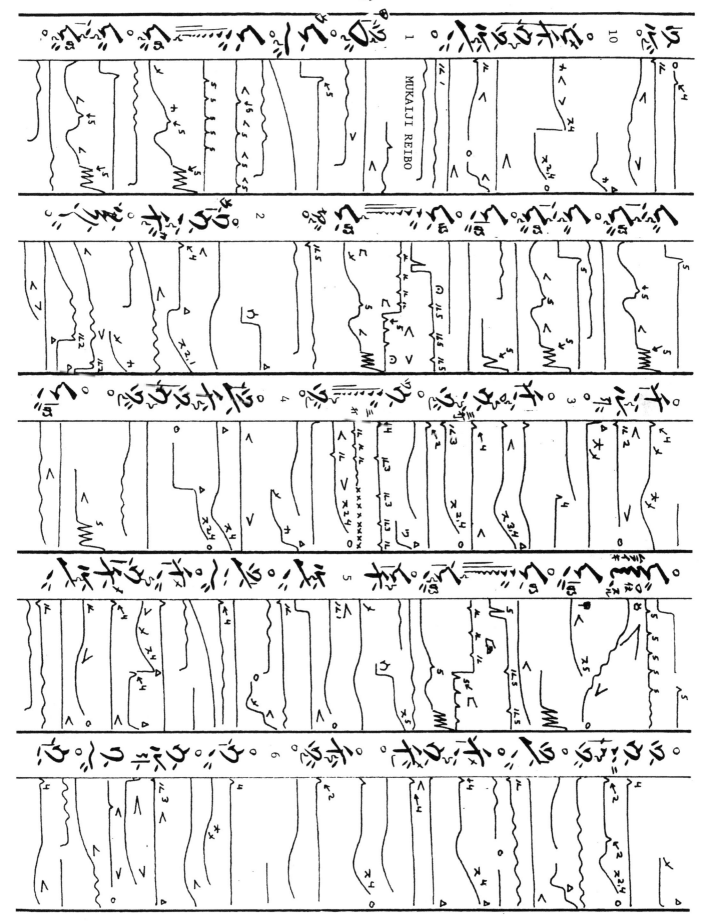

MUKAIJI REIBO

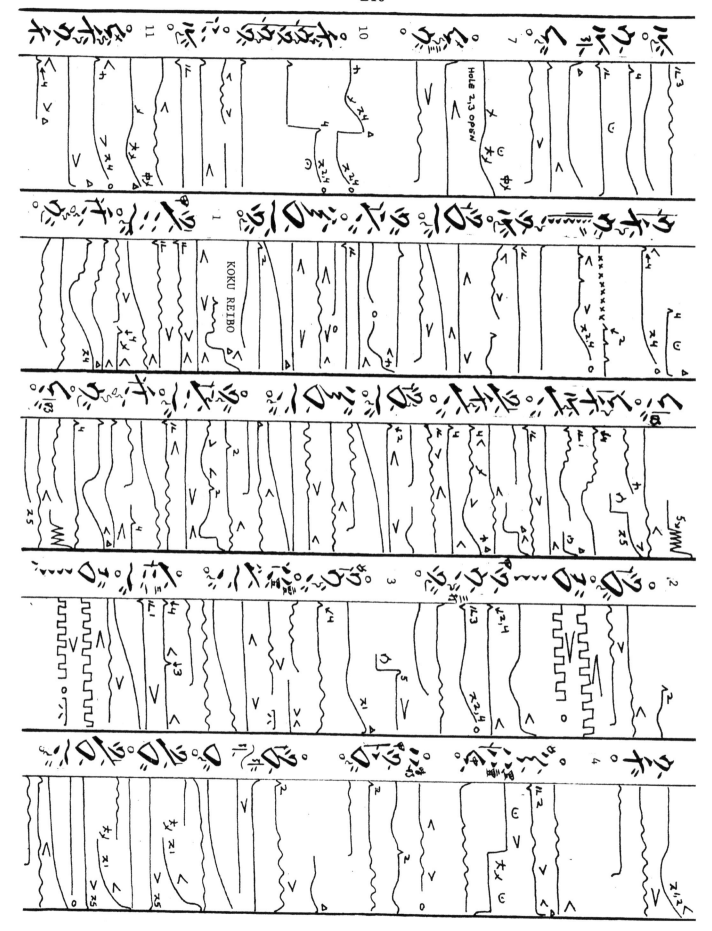

KOKU REIBO

Hole 2,3 OPEN

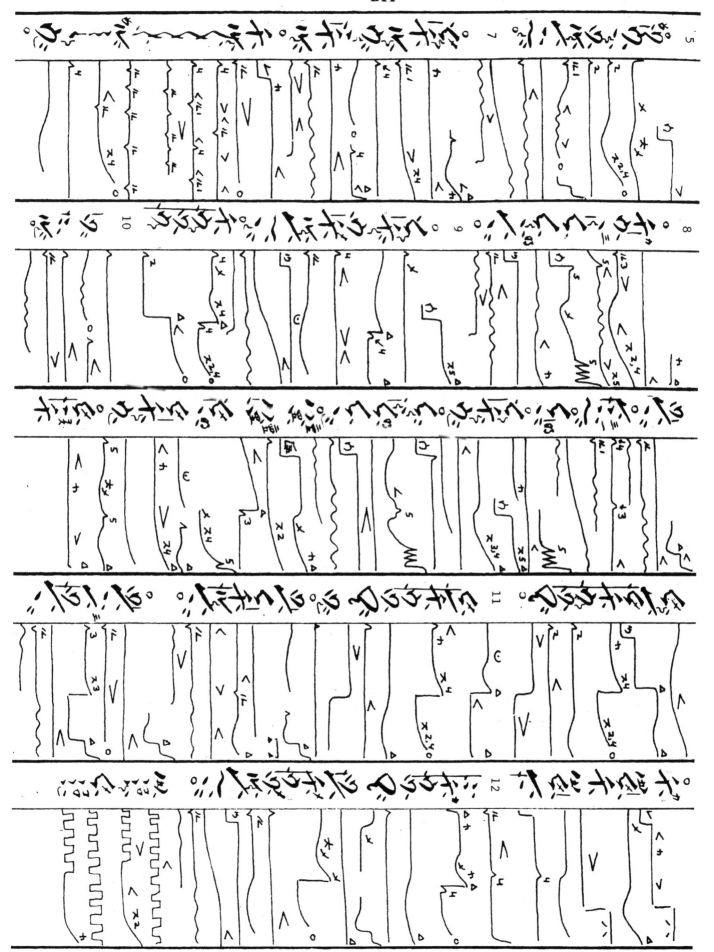

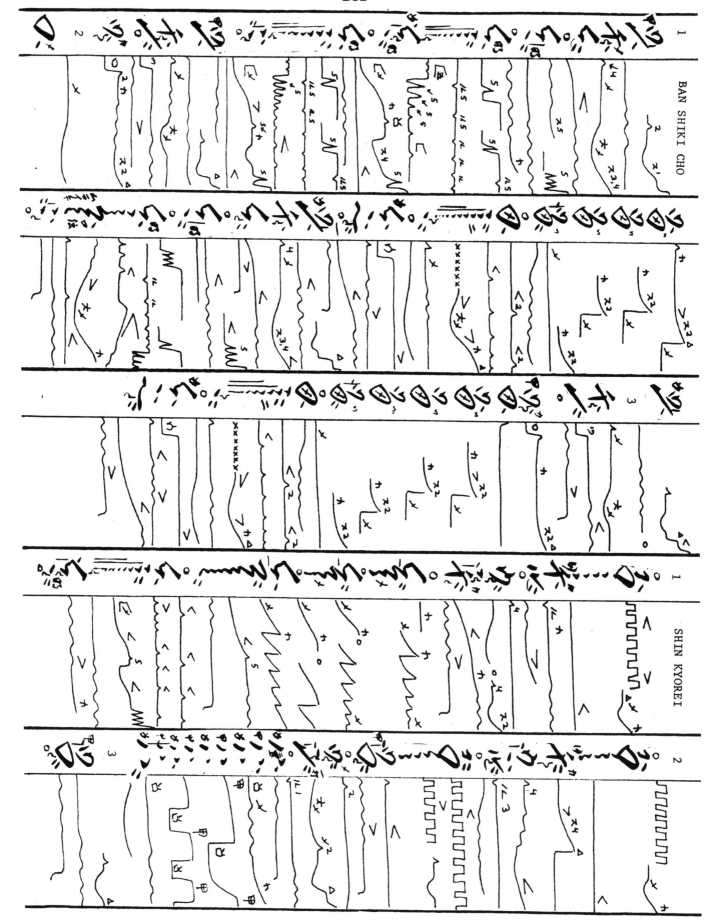

KOTO SAN KYOREI

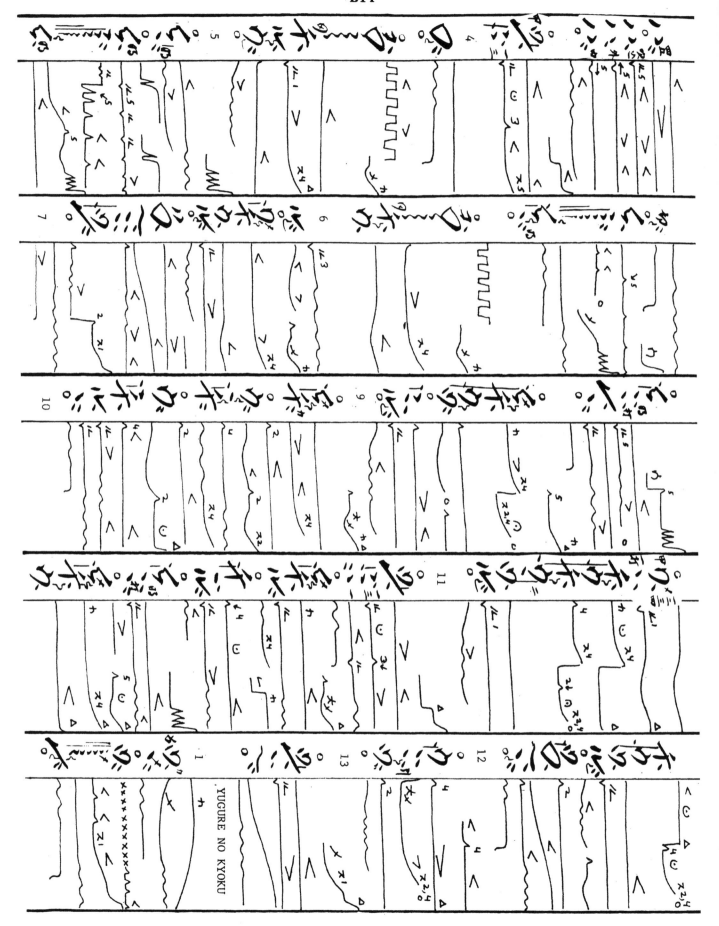

YUGURE NO KYOKU

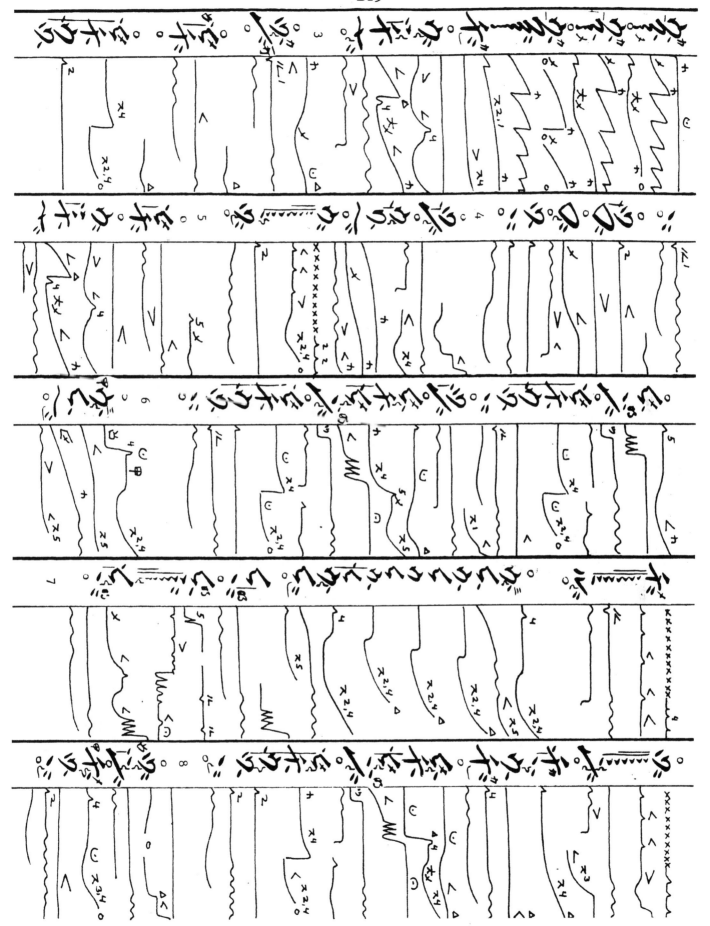

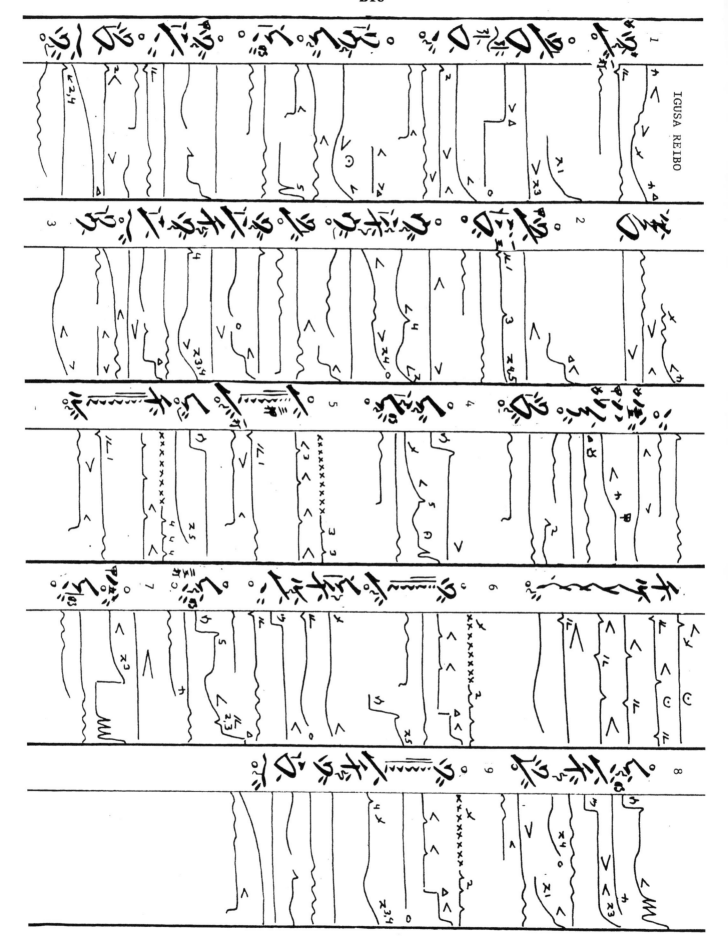

IGUSA REIBO

Printed in Great Britain
by Amazon

Carl and his sons gathering bamboo.

About The Author

Carl Abbott began Yoga in 1960 at the age of 17. At 19 he emigrated to Australia. Pursuing a deep inner quest he spent the next 15 years wandering and working in mostly in Asia, studying Yoga, Taoist and Buddhist philosophies and related disciplines: Hatha Yoga, Tai Chi, Karate, Zen and Shakuhachi.

In Japan, he studied Shakuhachi construction and playing with Kawase Junsuke II, Kawase Junsuke III, and Mr. Goro Yamaguchi, three respected masters of the Shakuhachi.

He returned to the United States and settled in California, where he lives with his wife and two sons. He is currently spokesman for CenterTao in Santa Cruz.

About CenterTao

The Center For Taoist Thought And Fellowship (a.k.a. Center-Tao), founded in 1982, is a California non-profit religious (Taoist) corporation. It is located at 406 Lincoln St., Santa Cruz, CA 95060.

A Taoist meeting is held the first Sunday of every month at 10 a.m. The general public is welcome. The hour long meeting is divided into 3 parts, each divided by the ringing of a bell.

The service begins with a short silent period, followed by a reading from the Tao Te Ching. Those who wish discuss the verse and what it means to them personally. The service concludes with another short silent period.

The first verse of the Tao Te Ching illustrates the humility we endeavor to bring to the service:

> *The way that can be told, is not the constant way;*
> *The name that can be named, is not the constant name.*

Other Offerings

Blowing Zen After covering basic information and history background you'll be guided step-by-step from producing sound and playing simple folk tunes to playing Buddhist Meditation music.

This book combined with the free online video lessons at Centertao.org/learn-zen will take you from absolute zero to Honkyoku (Zen Buddhist meditation through the shakuhachi flute).

There is also detailed information on making two types of Shakuhachi: a simple plastic pipe version and the traditional tapered bore root bamboo version.

Blowing Zen: Expanded Edition is two books in one. The first is the original Blowing Zen (see details above). The 'Expanded' section is Blowing Zen II (this book) Note, the Expanded Edition includes the 72 minute CD (see below).

The companion CD sold with the Expanded Edition or available at Toneway.com/products/blowing-zen as an MP3 download, contains the Japanese folk tunes, chamber music and Buddhist composition "Hi Fu Mi" taught in the first section of the book. It also includes examples of timing and standard Buddhist music phrases. (Note: the online video lessons cover the same material as on the CD, albeit in video format).

The **Yuu Shakuhachi** is made from high quality plastic. This flute while lacking the genuine look and feel of bamboo, comes very close. Most importantly, it plays and sound better than bamboo flutes costing much more. Perfect for seeing if the Shakuhachi is right for you. Another important advantage, it won't crack! Take it to the mountains; taket it to the beach; take it to work. Go to Toneway.com/products/blowing-zen for more information.

Hatha Yoga: The Essential Dynamics guides you step by step from beginning through advanced Yoga using vectorial information for 138 postures as taught by B.K.S. Iyengar.

The full page, large print format enables you to learn (or remember) at a glance, what you need to be doing while your are doing it. You can preview this book at Centertao.org/yoga-book.

Tao Te Ching, Word for Word is a more literal translation of this Taoist classic. First, I give a poetic rendering of the chapter. This is followed by a word-for-word, line-by-line translation of the Chinese.

Using these to cross check frequently with one's favorite English translation can deepen one's understanding. Translations invariably lose some degree of the ancient 'original intention' due to the modern cultural context we bring to our language's words… our 'education'. The word-for-word section provides the many related synonym-like meaning with which the reader can use to piece together something closer to the original.

The second half of the book includes extensive commentary that relates each chapter to various aspects of life. Preview this book at Centertao.org/tao-book.

"Shamisen of Japan" teaches you how to professionally play and make the Tsugaru Shamisen, simply and enjoyably! It's really two books in one:

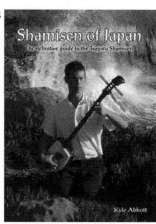

Included are step-by-step instructions for building your own shamisen, and a learning guide for playing shamisen, including notation for 16 traditional shamisen pieces. It is a valuable resource for both the beginner and the shamisen enthusiast! Learn about shamisen, watch the free shamisen crash course, and join the growing shamisen community at Bachido.com.

• • • • • •

If you have any questions e-mail us at Centertao.org or write CenterTao, 406 Lincoln St., Santa Cruz, CA. 95060 for more information.

新高砂

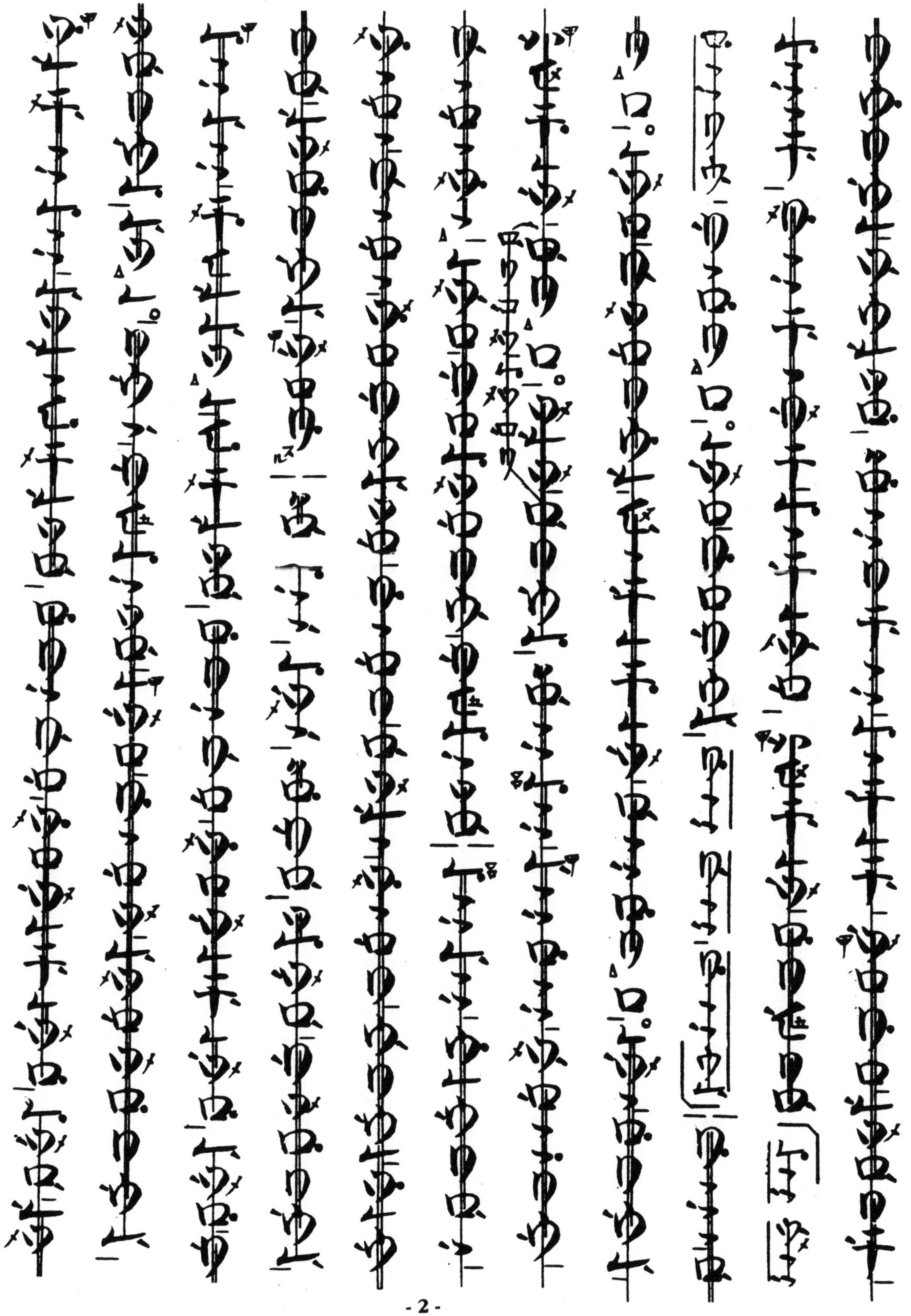

摘草

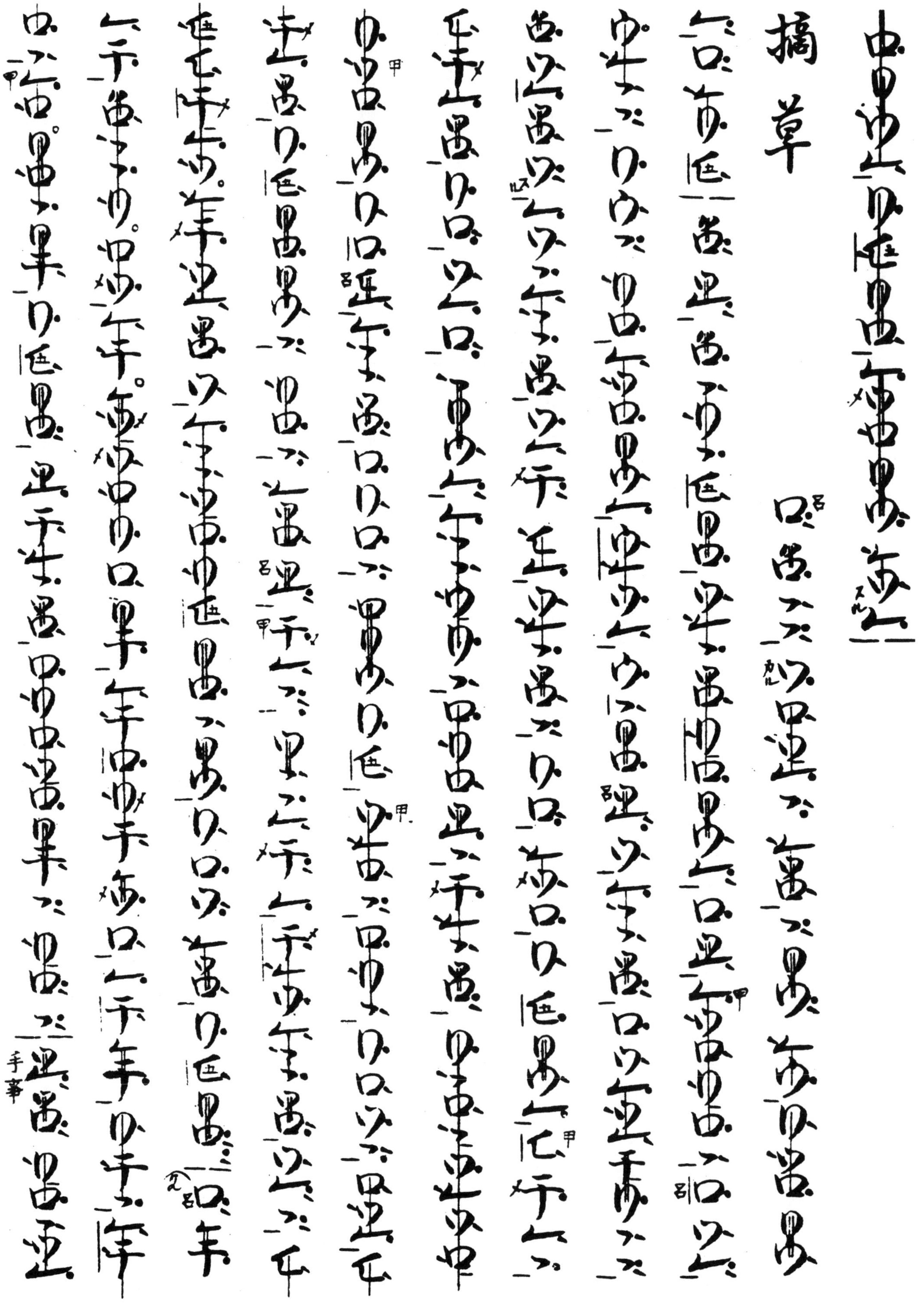

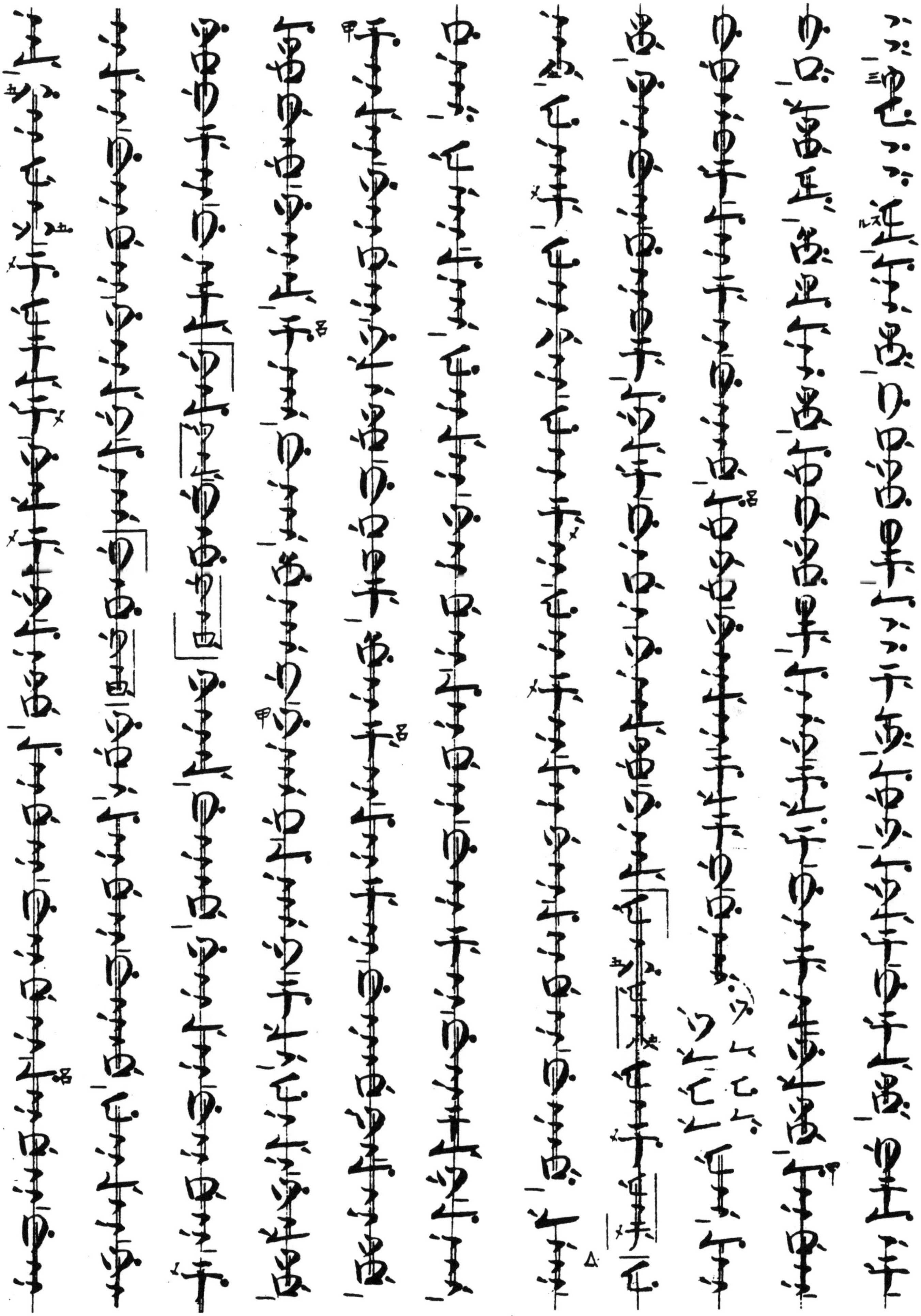

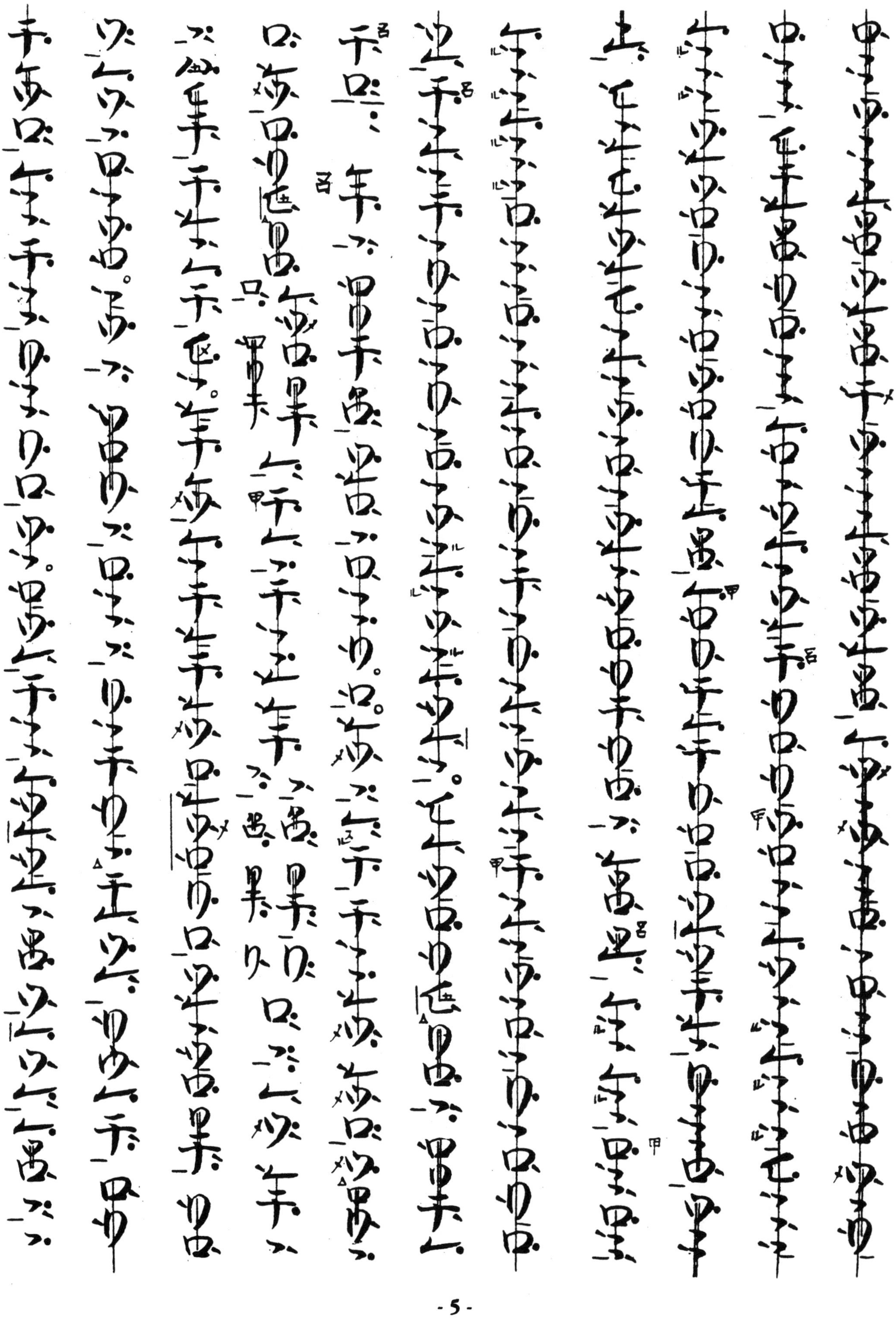

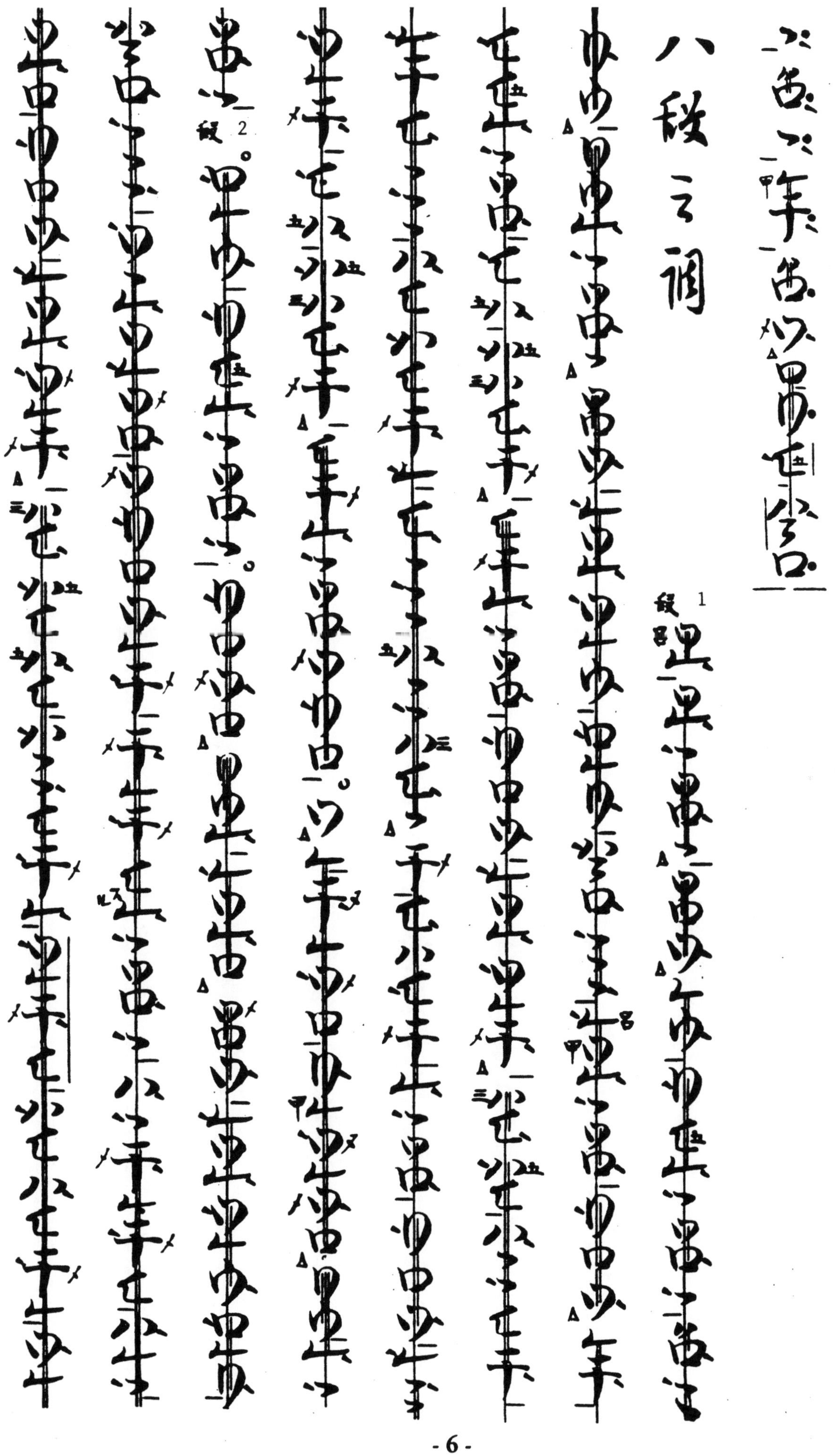
八段之調

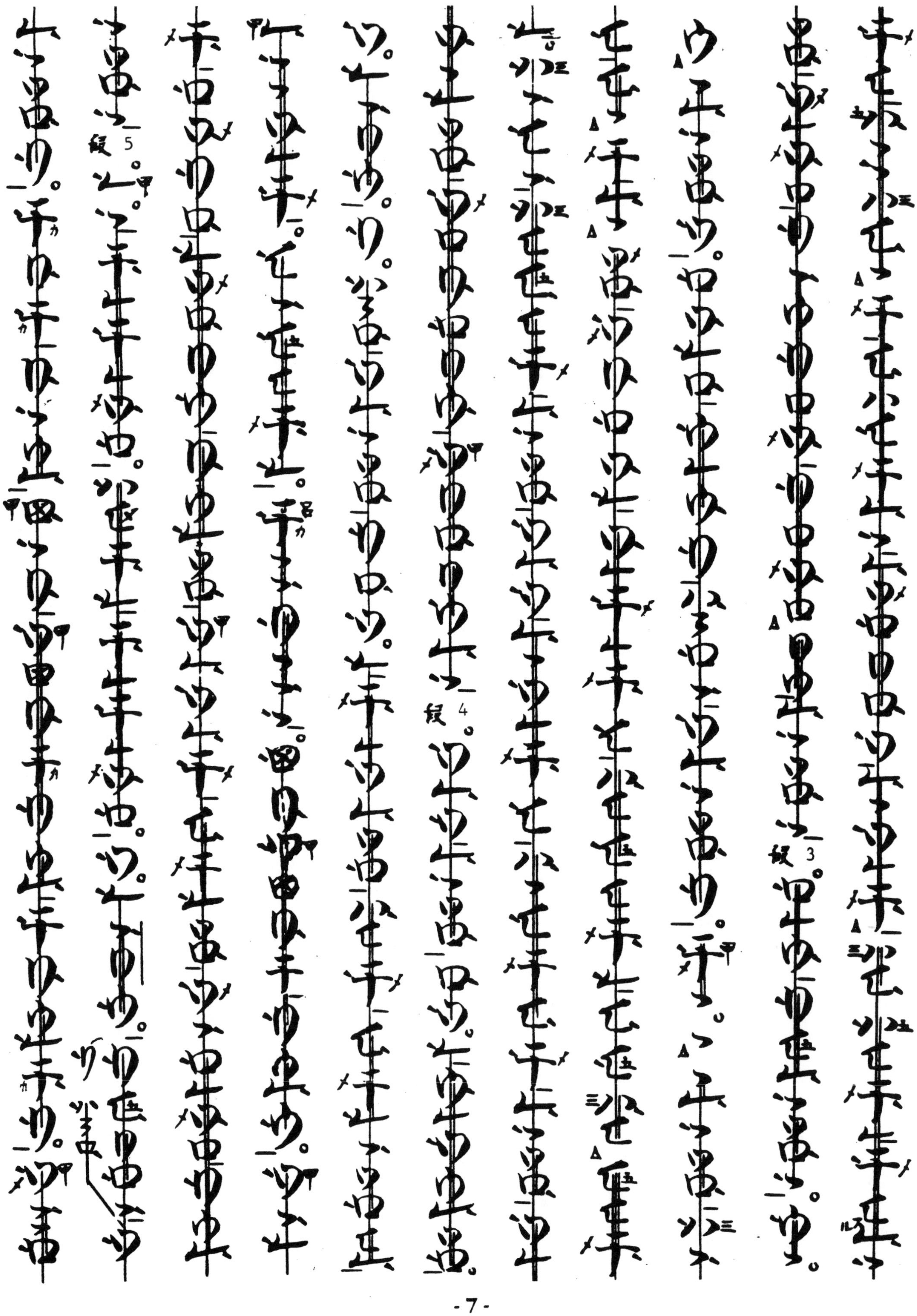

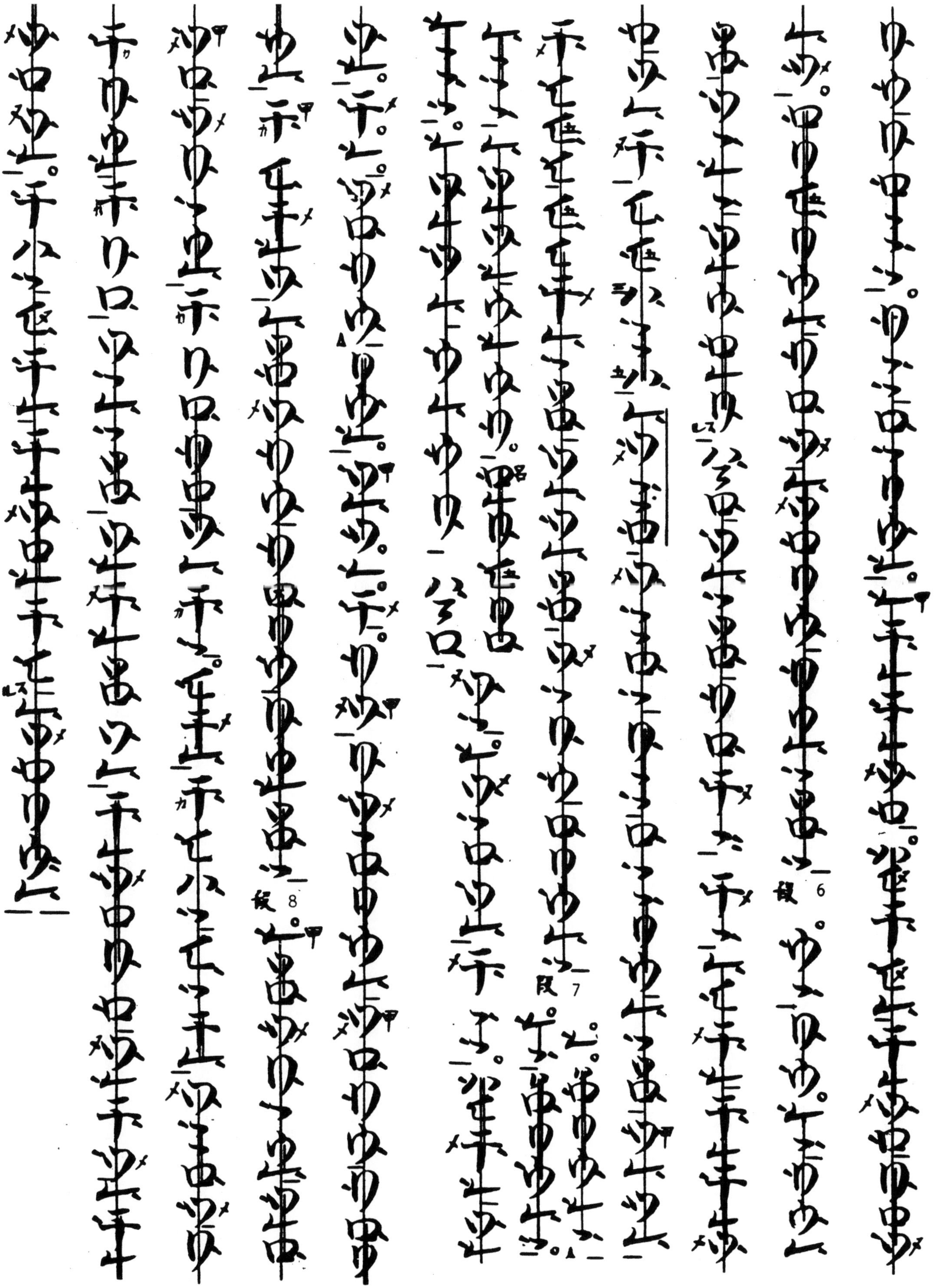
段 6
段 7
段 8

茶湯音頭

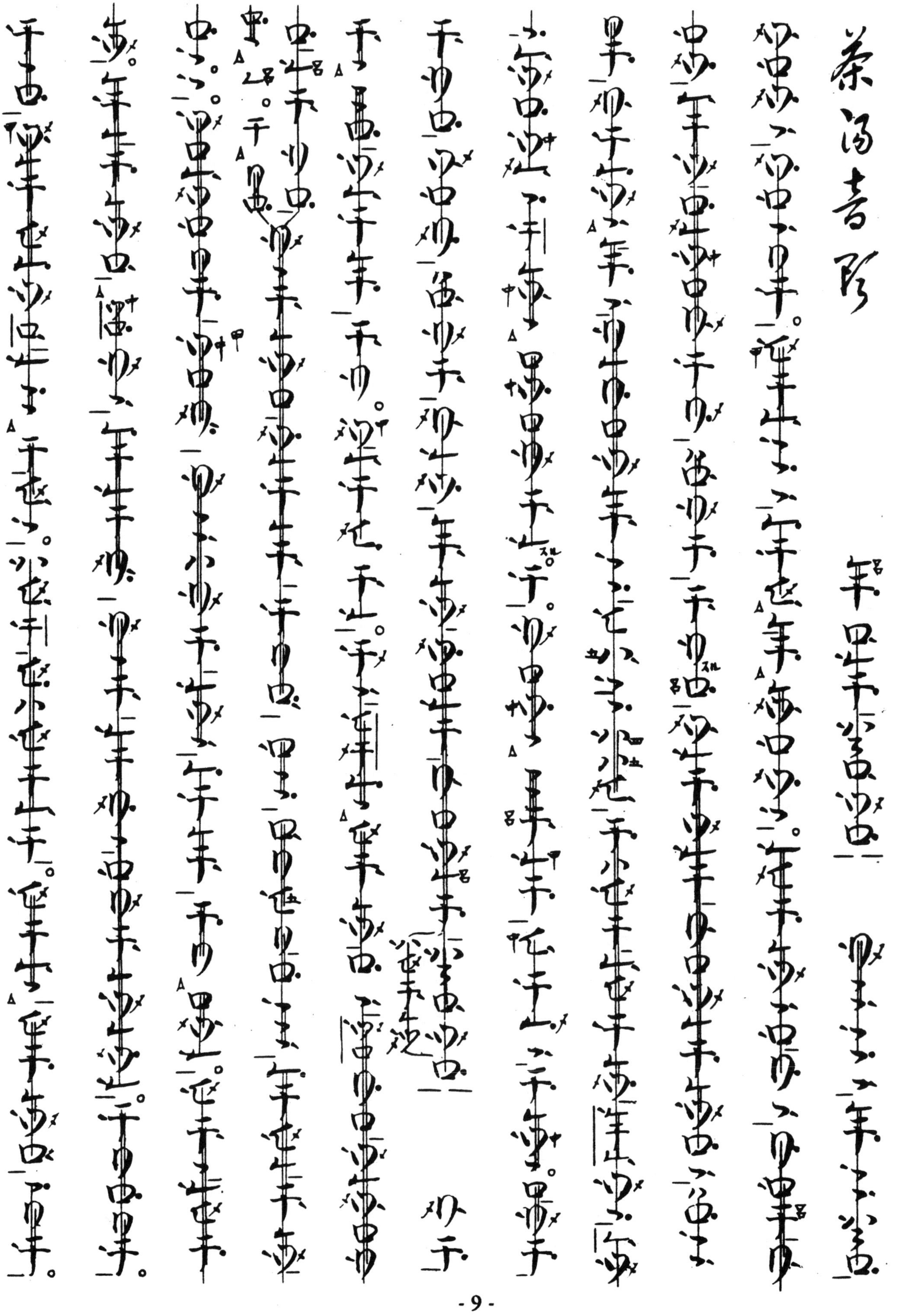

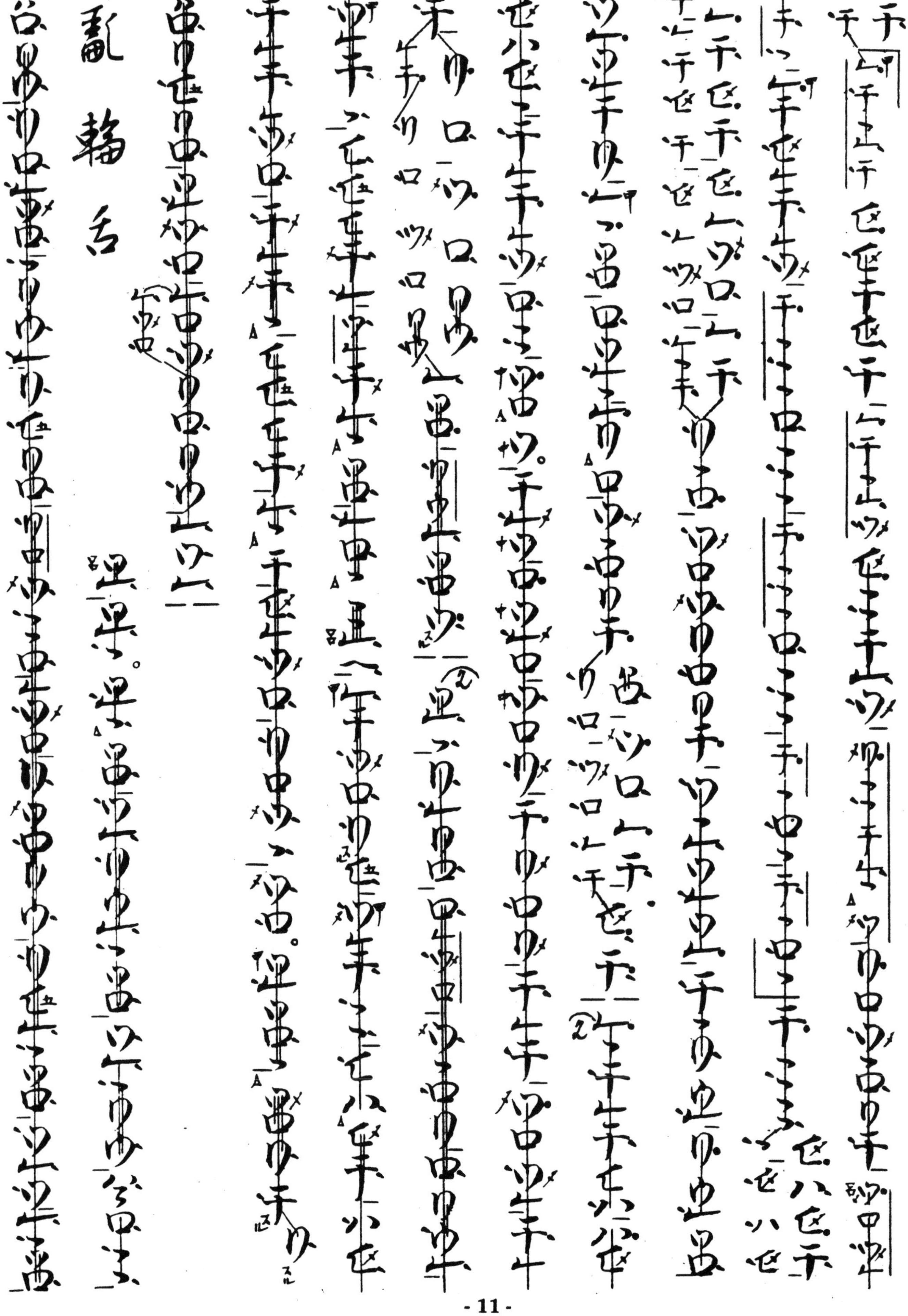
亂輪舌

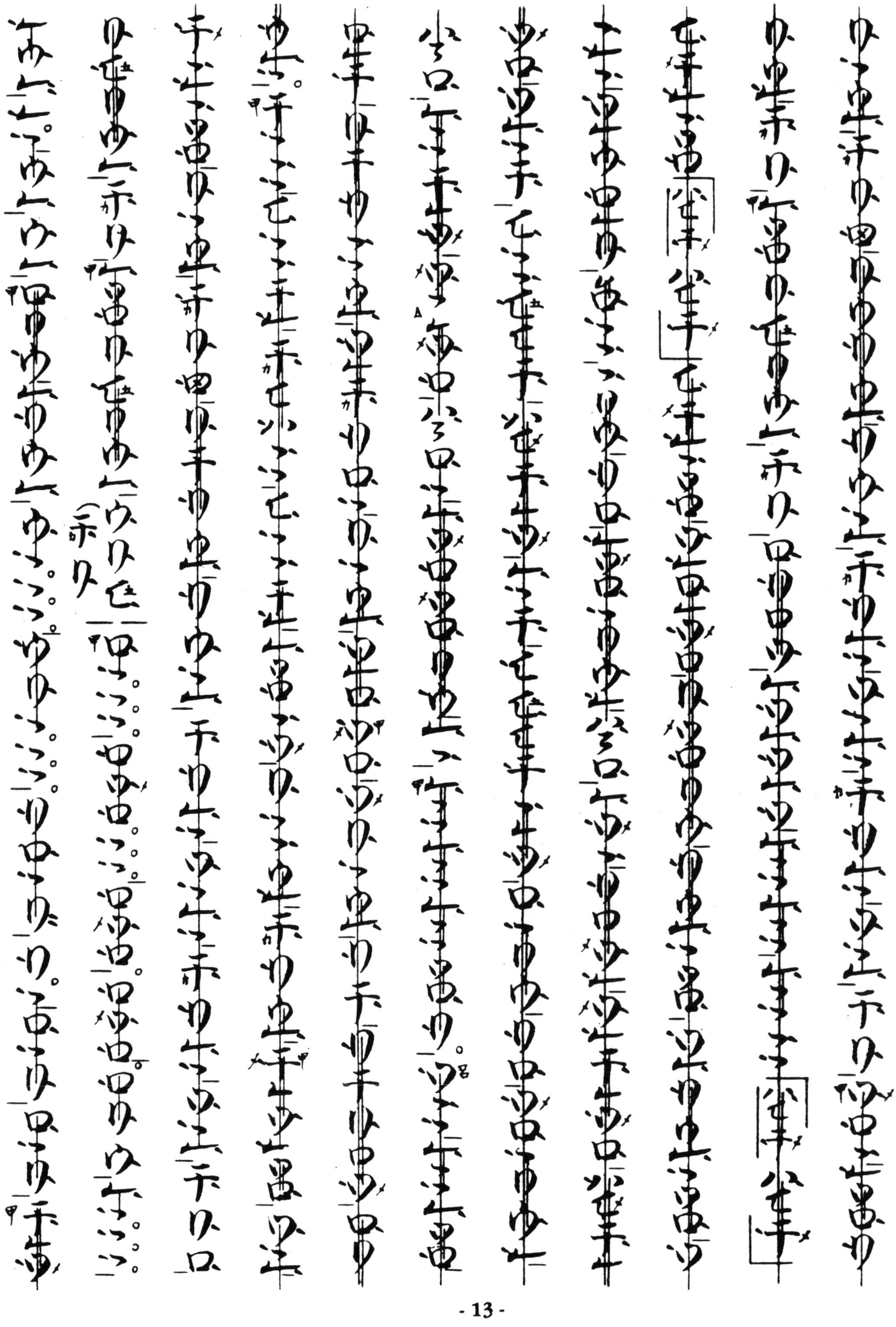

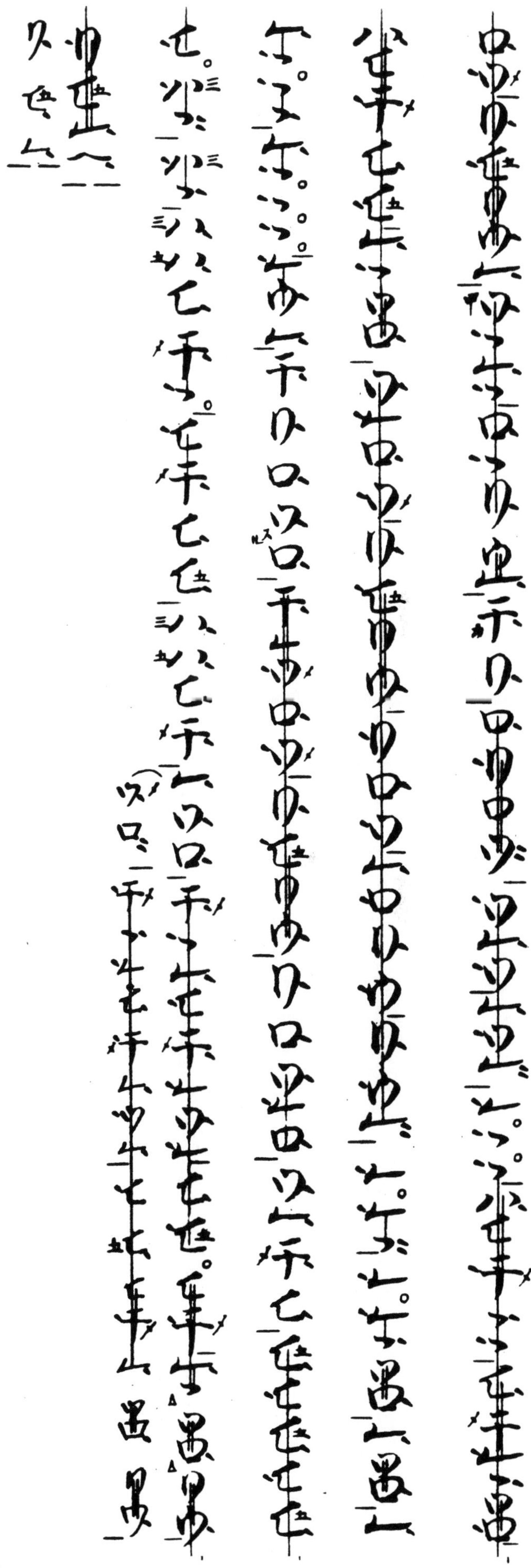

瀧落の曲

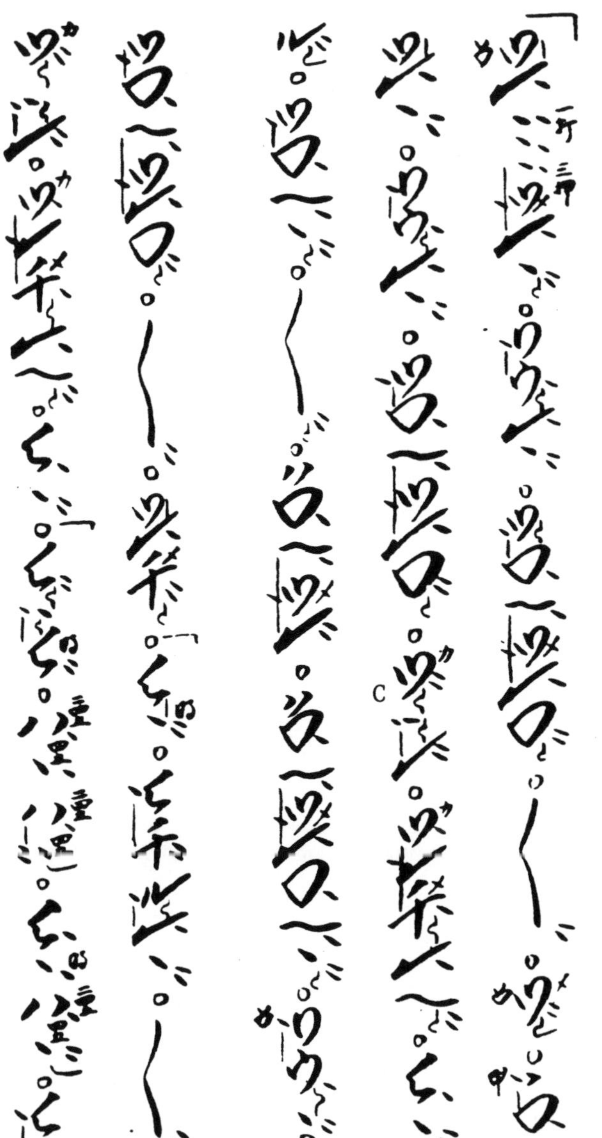

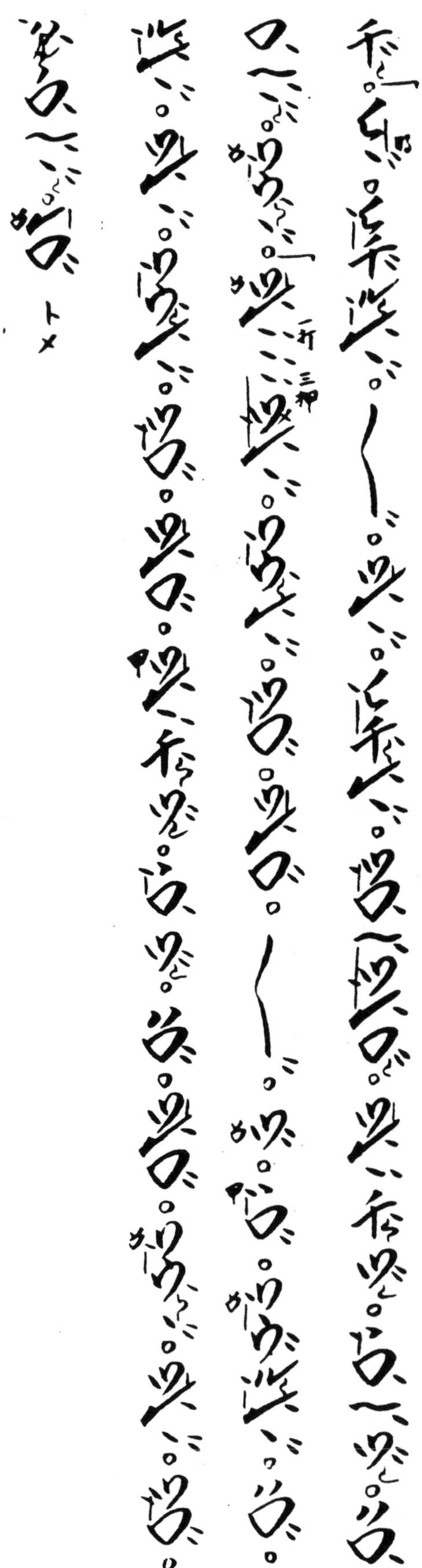

秋田菅垣

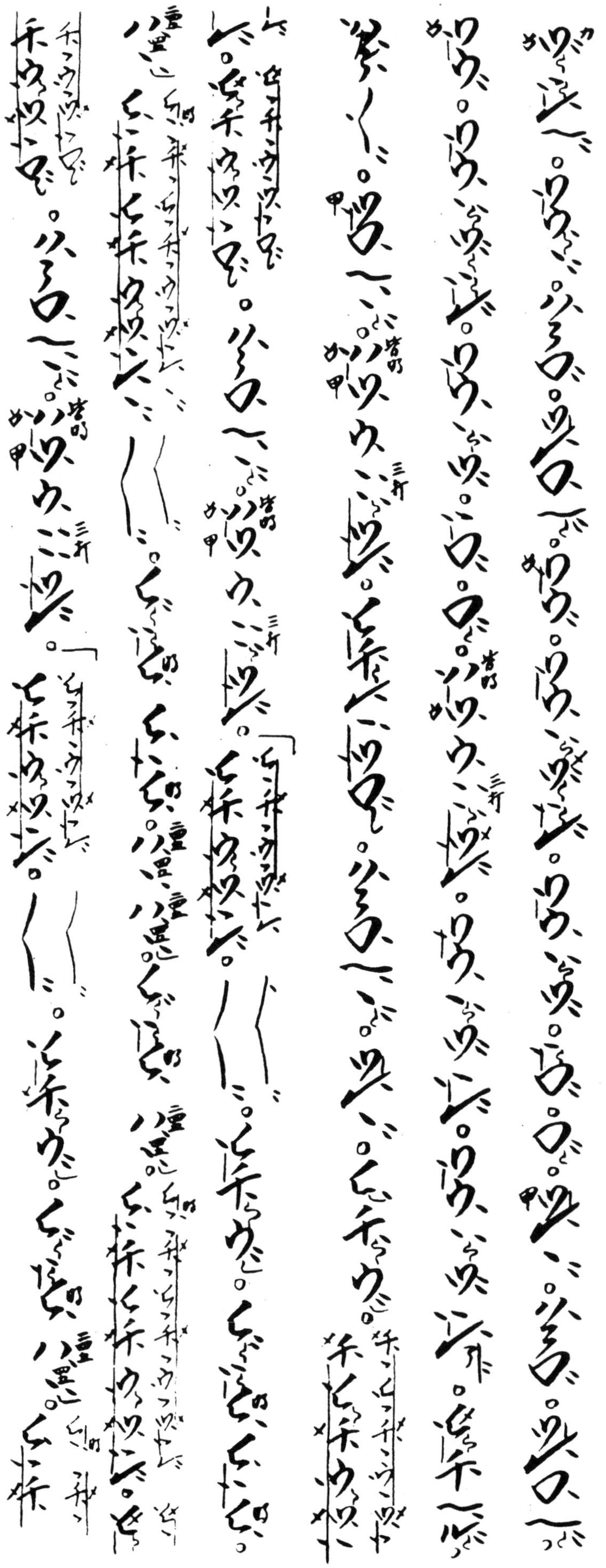

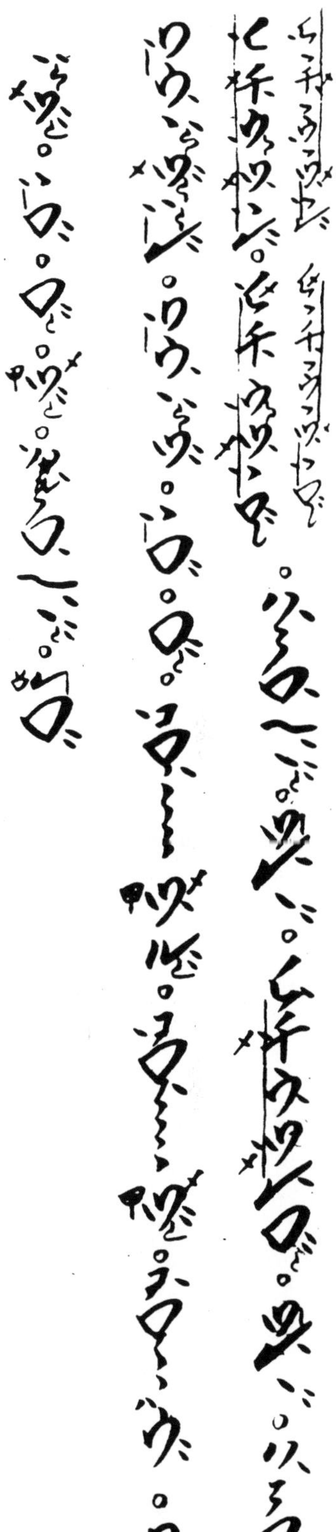

九州鈴慕

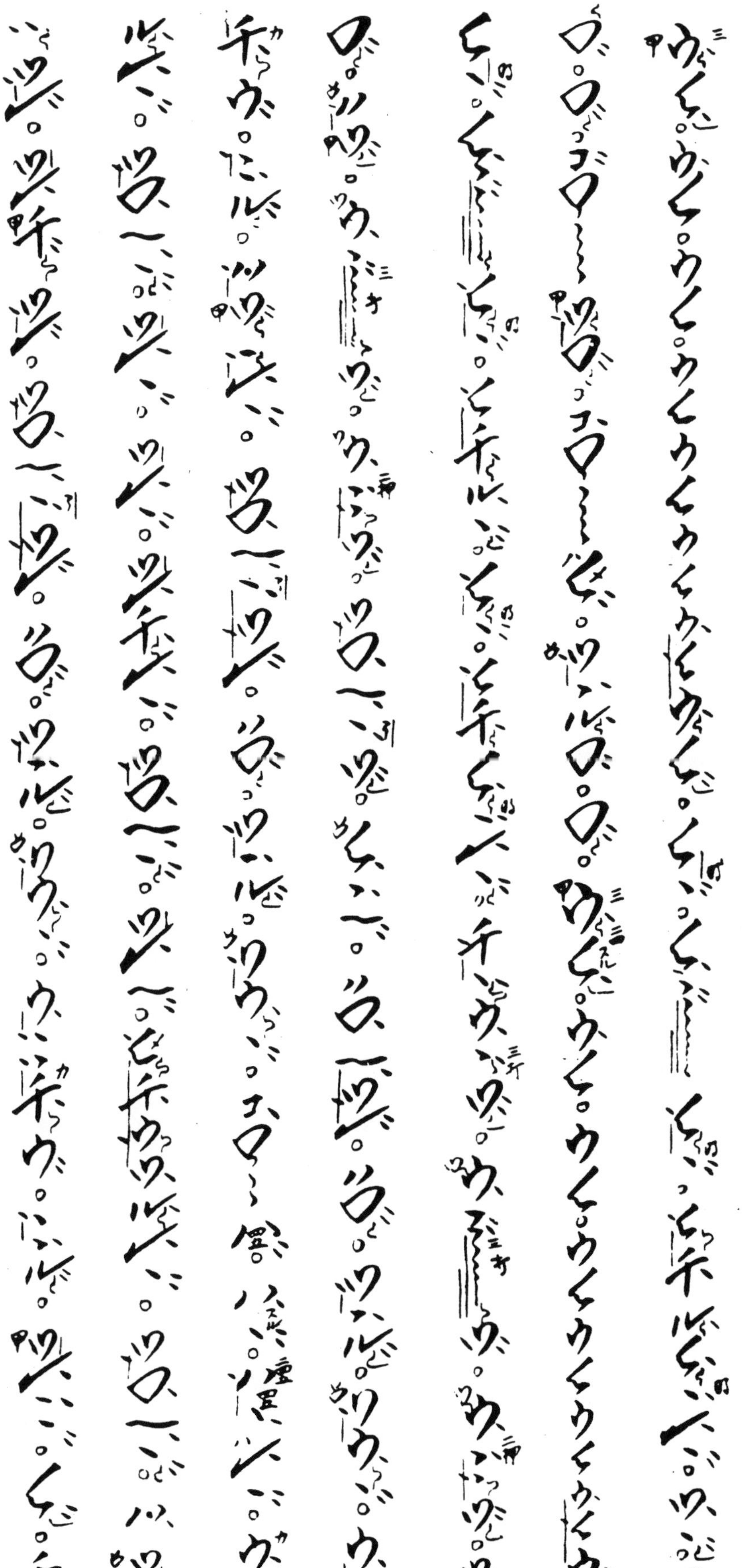

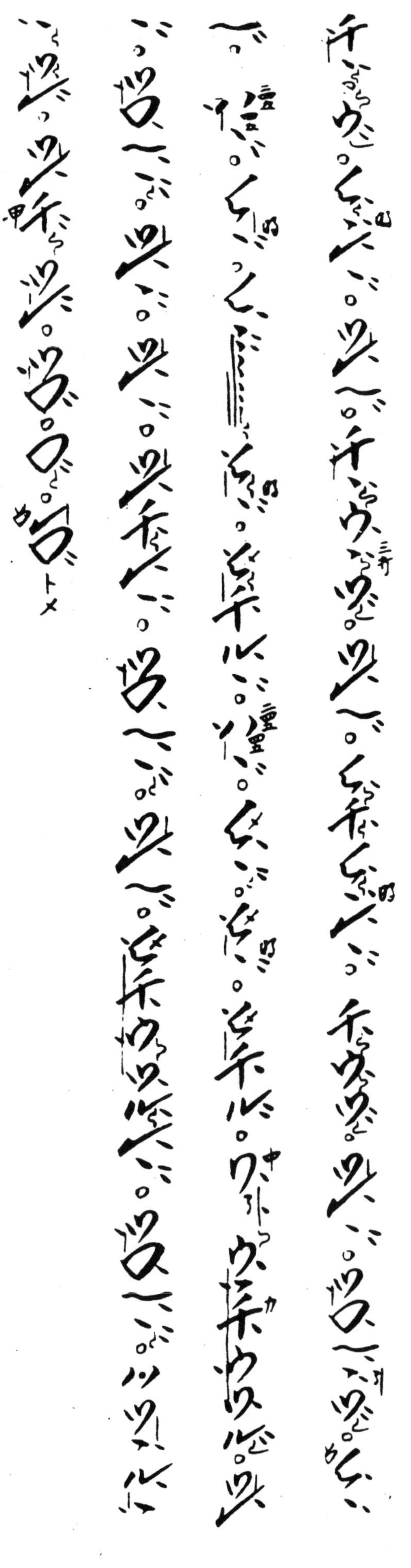

霧海篪鈴慕

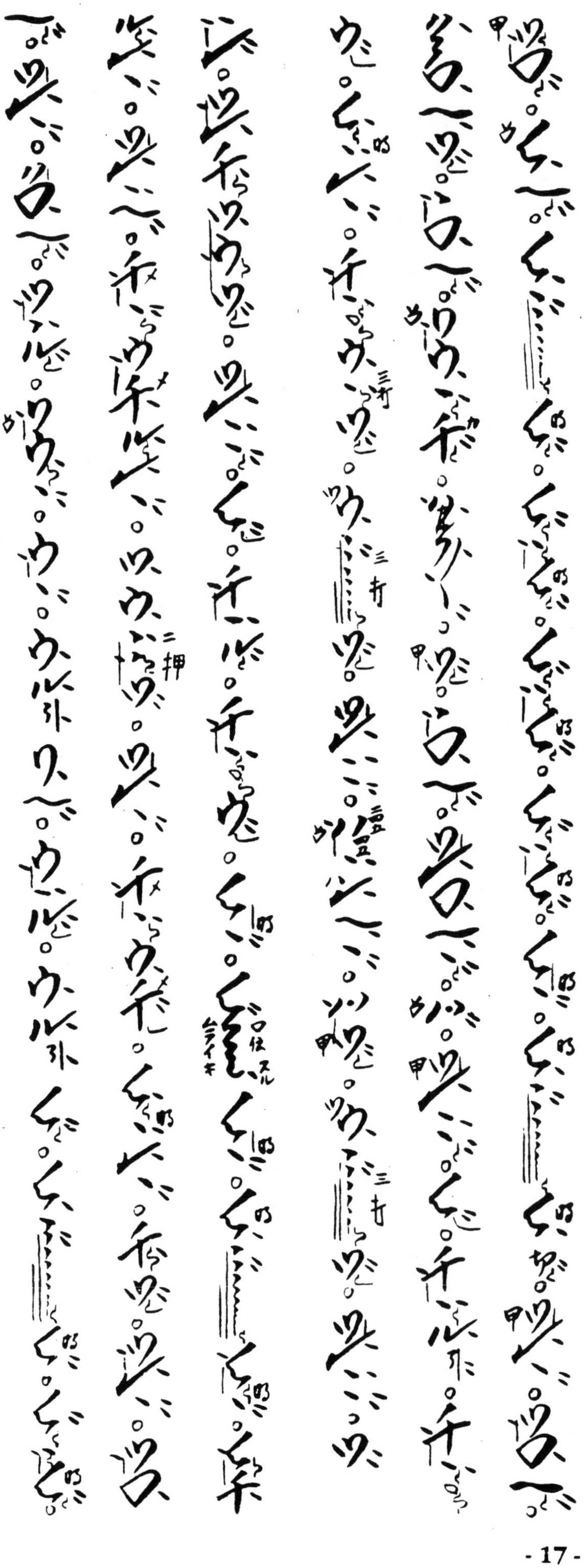

霧空鈴慕

盤　湯　諷

琴三虚霊

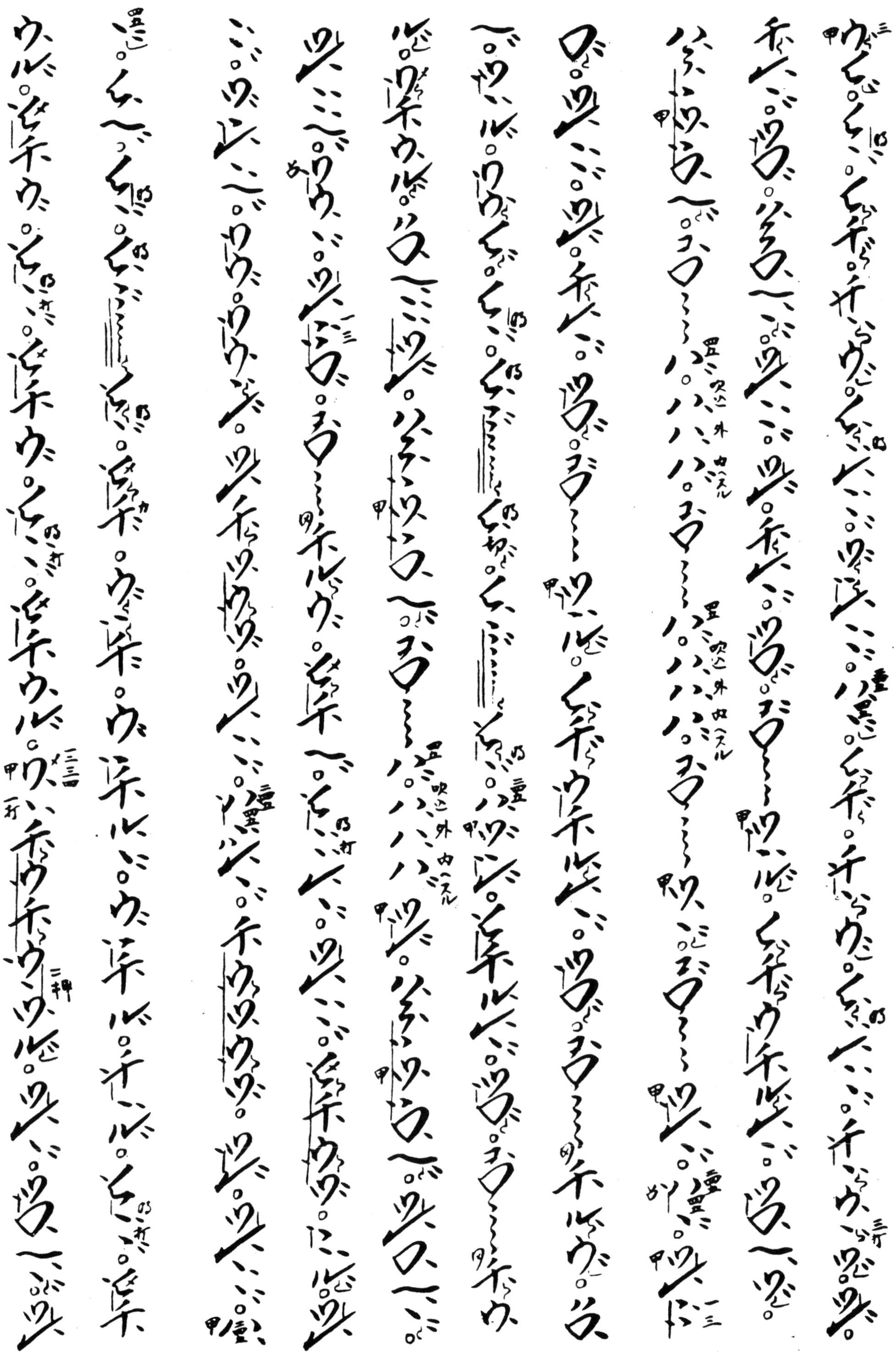

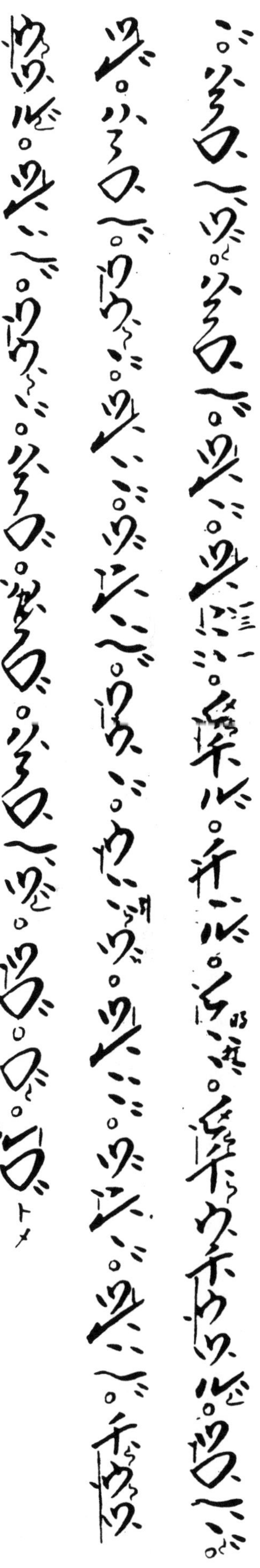

夕暮の曲

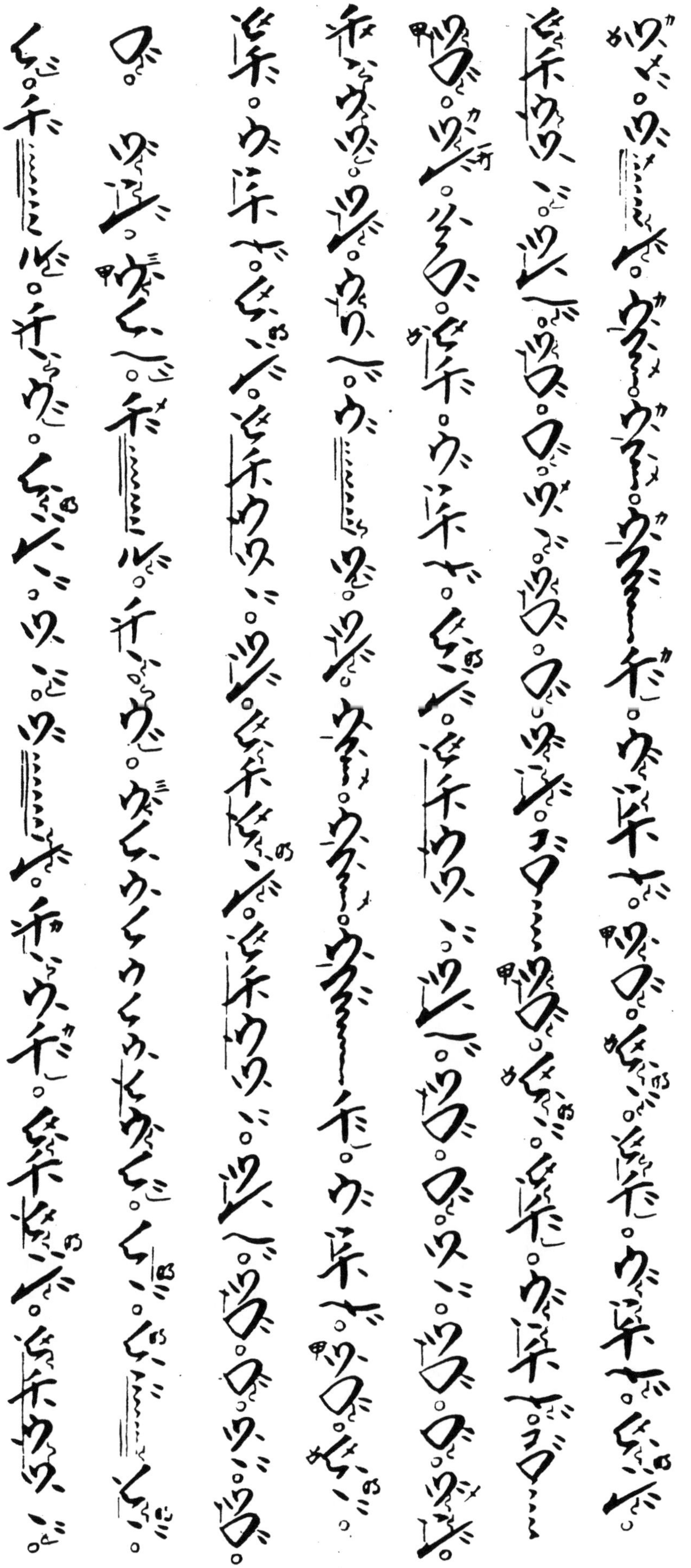

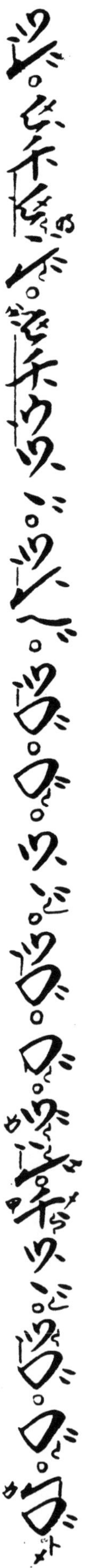

葦草鈴慕

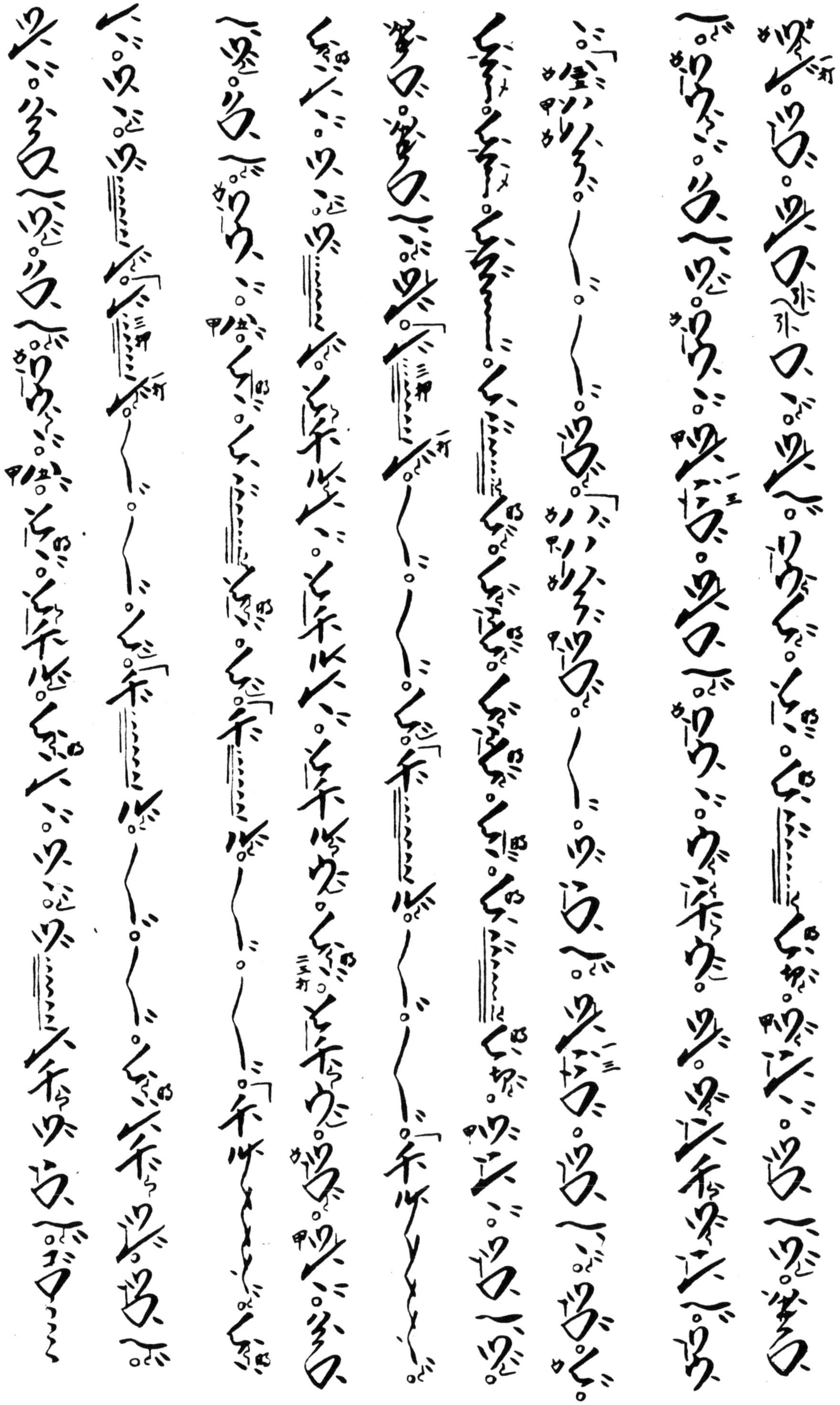

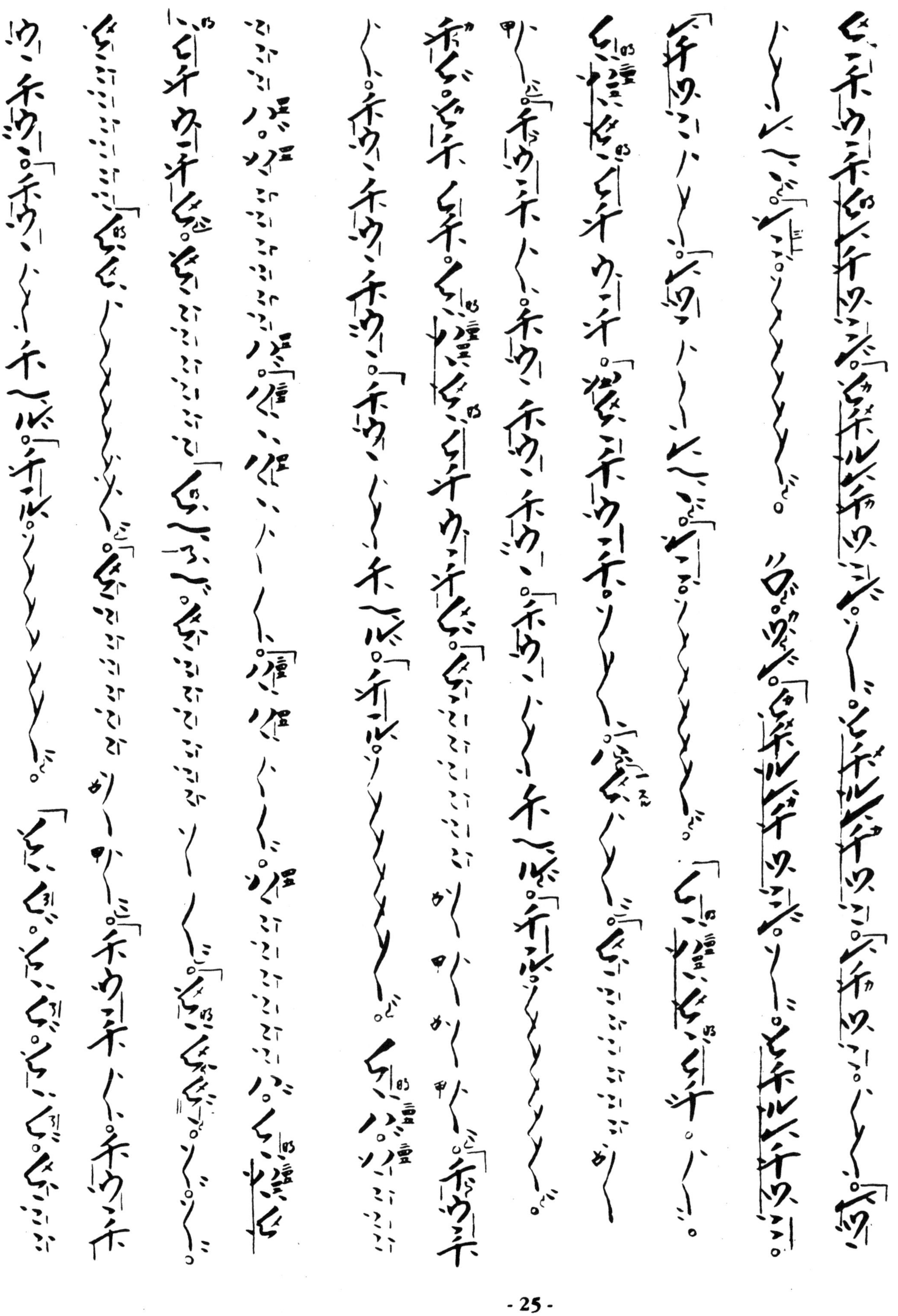

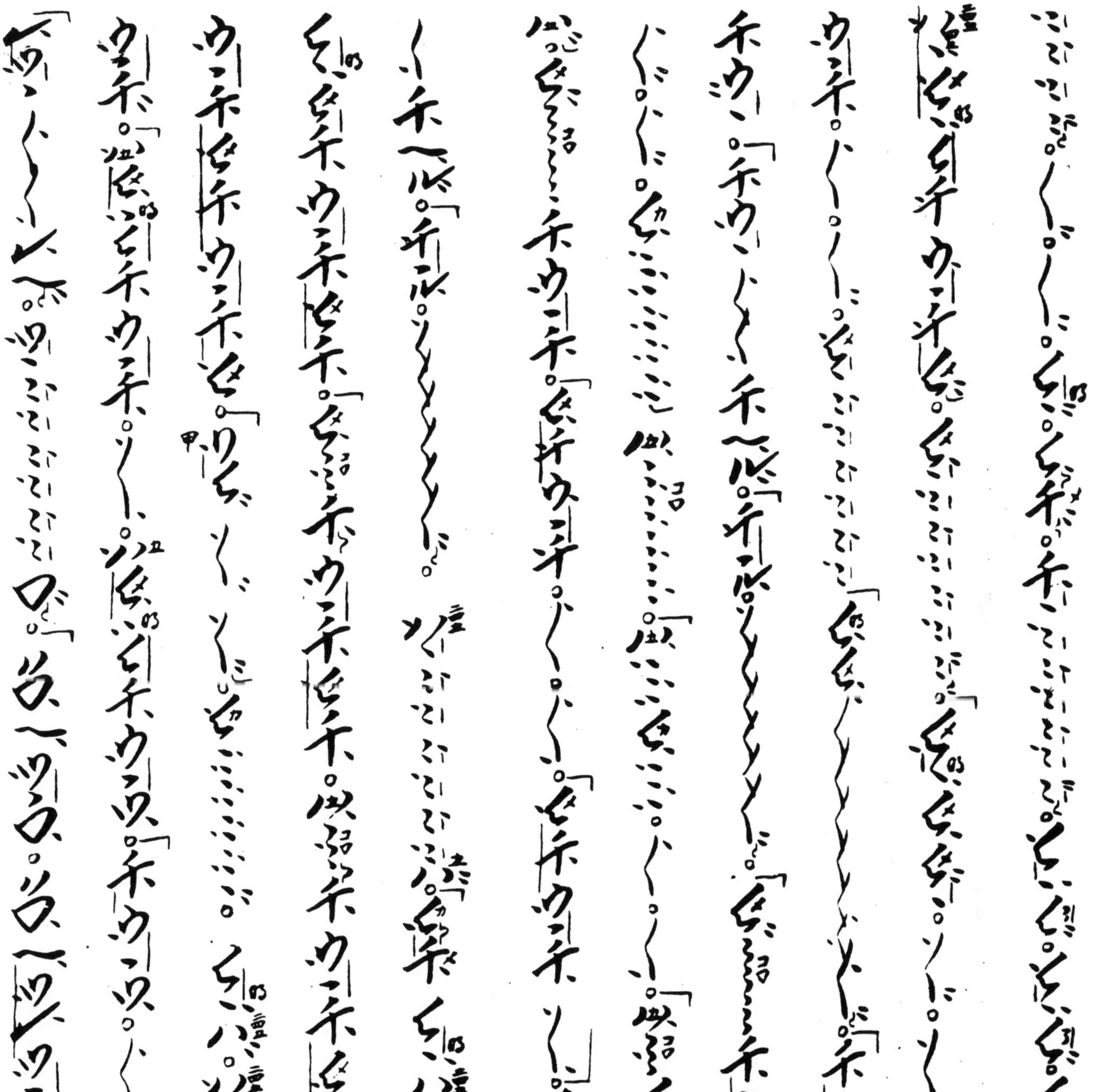

下り葉の曲

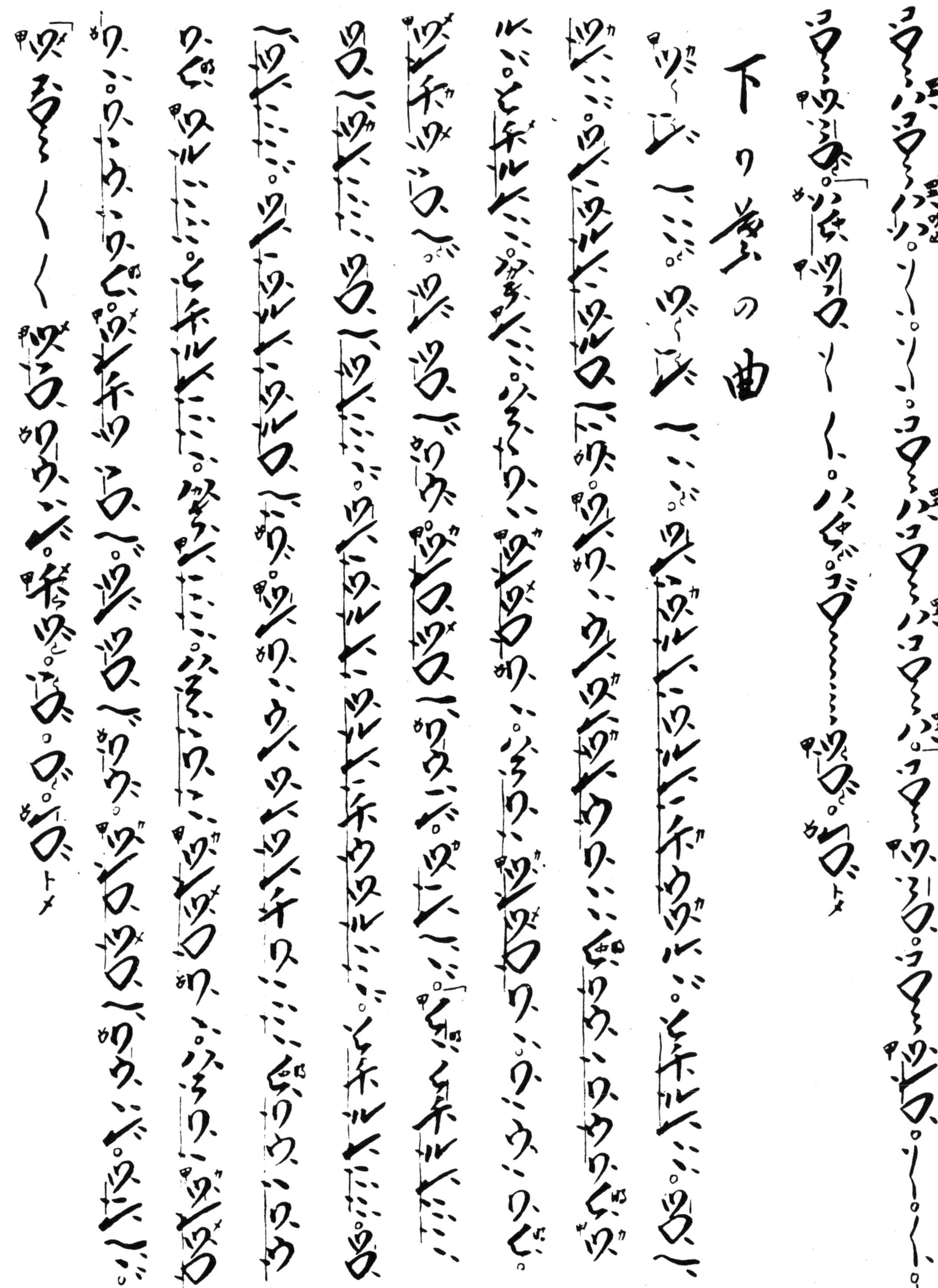

鹿の遠音

雲井 獅子

- 29 -

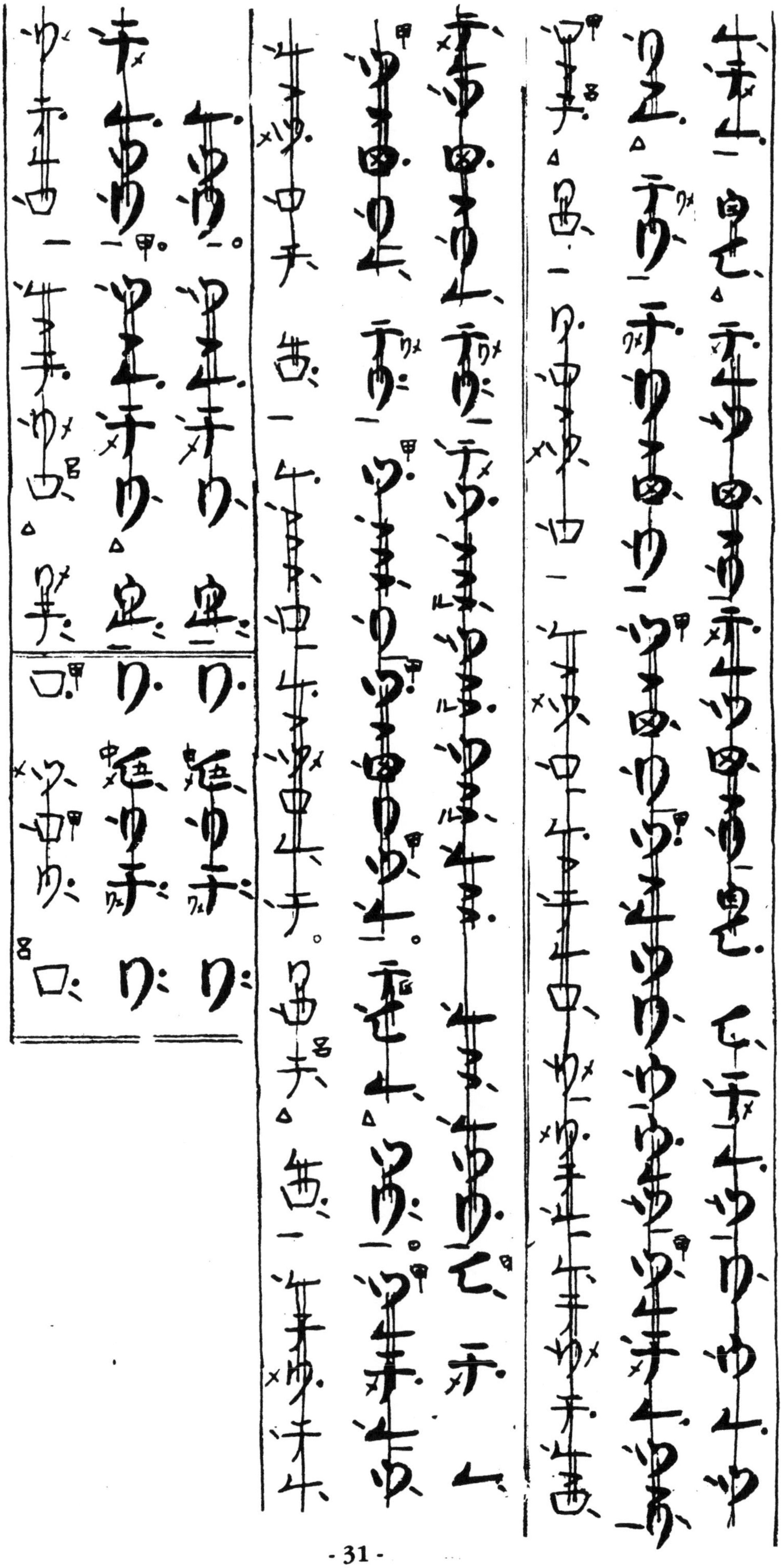

雲井獅子

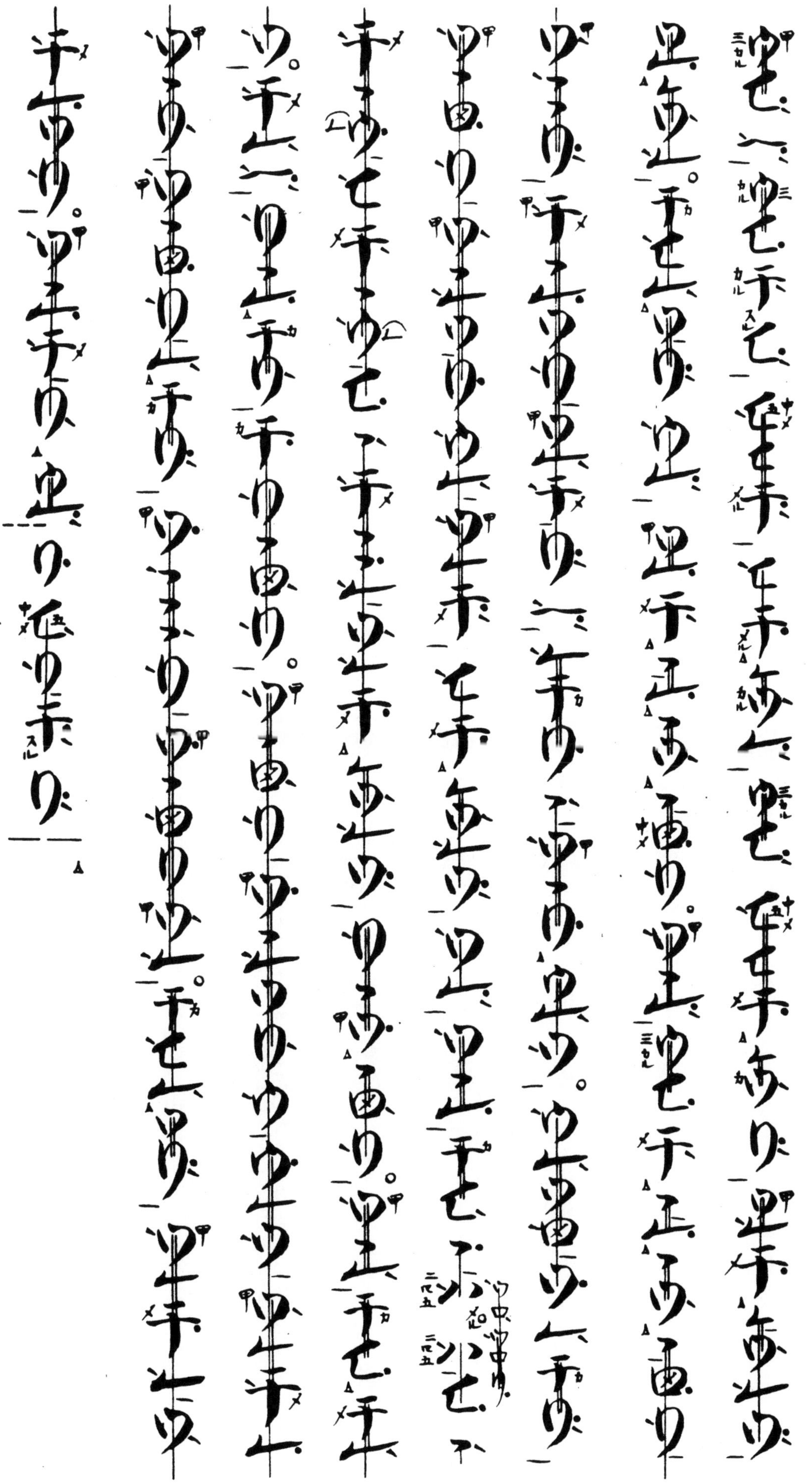

佟山菱垣

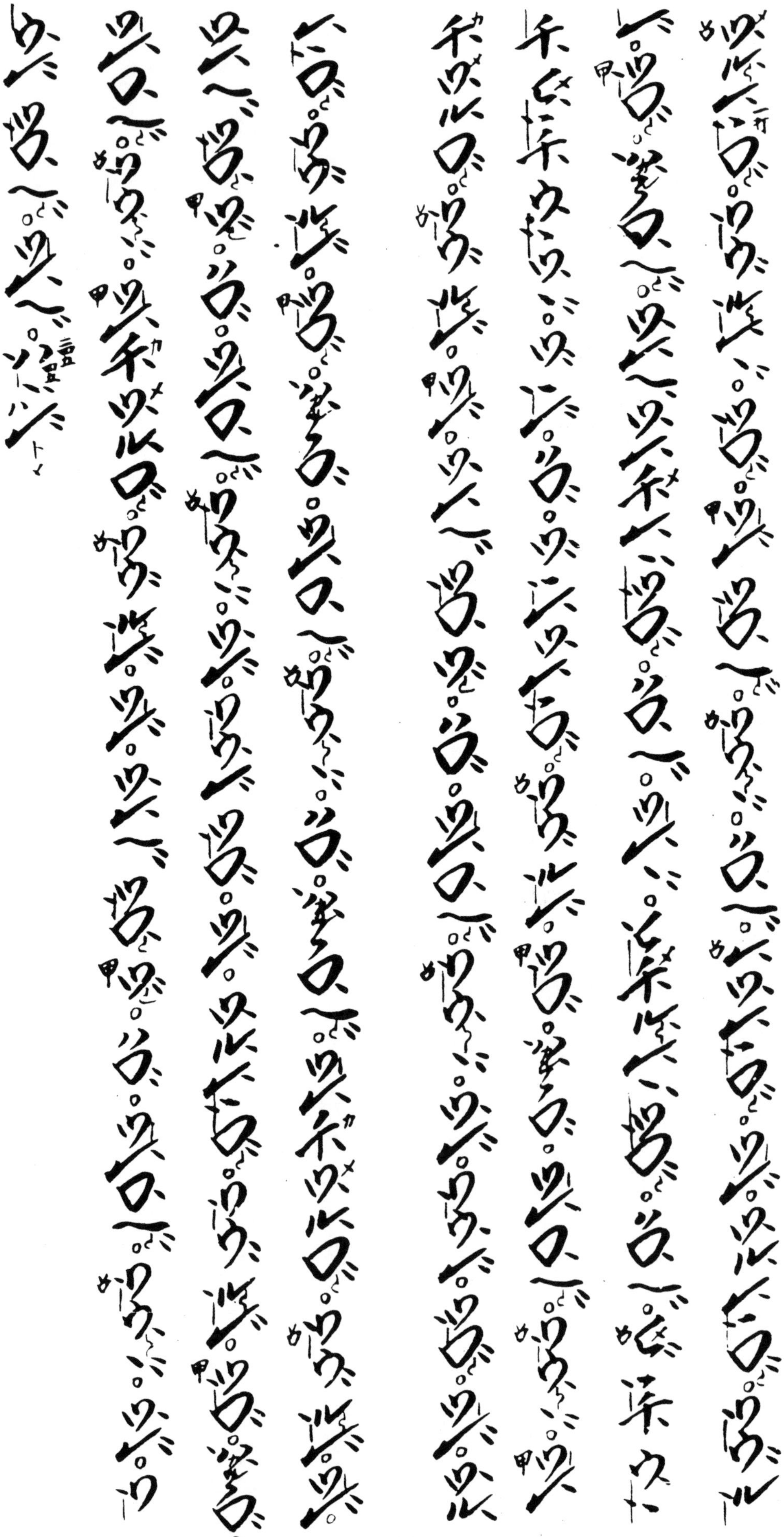

月の曲

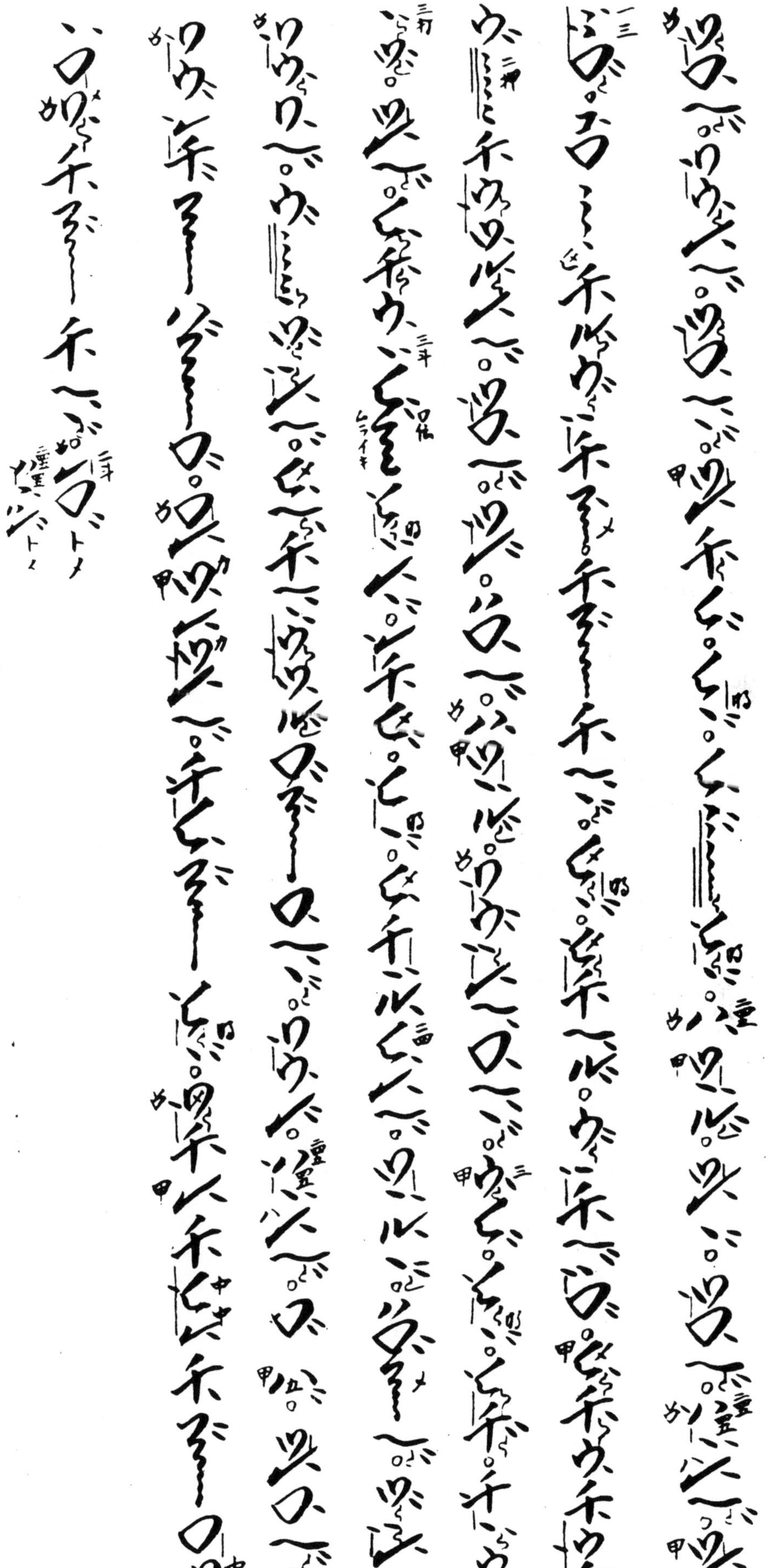

吾妻獅子

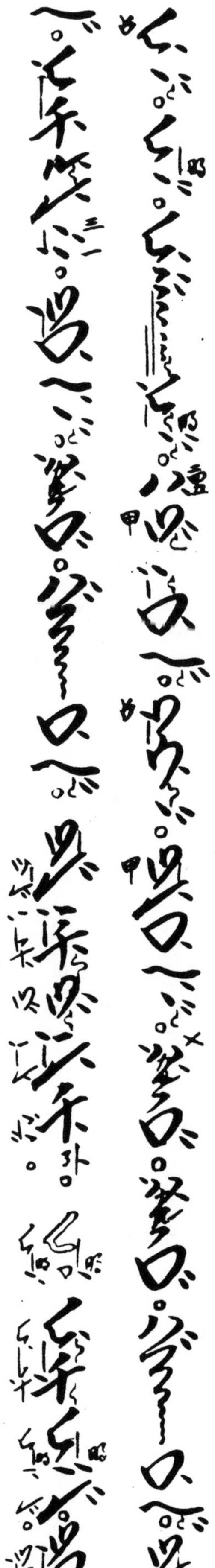

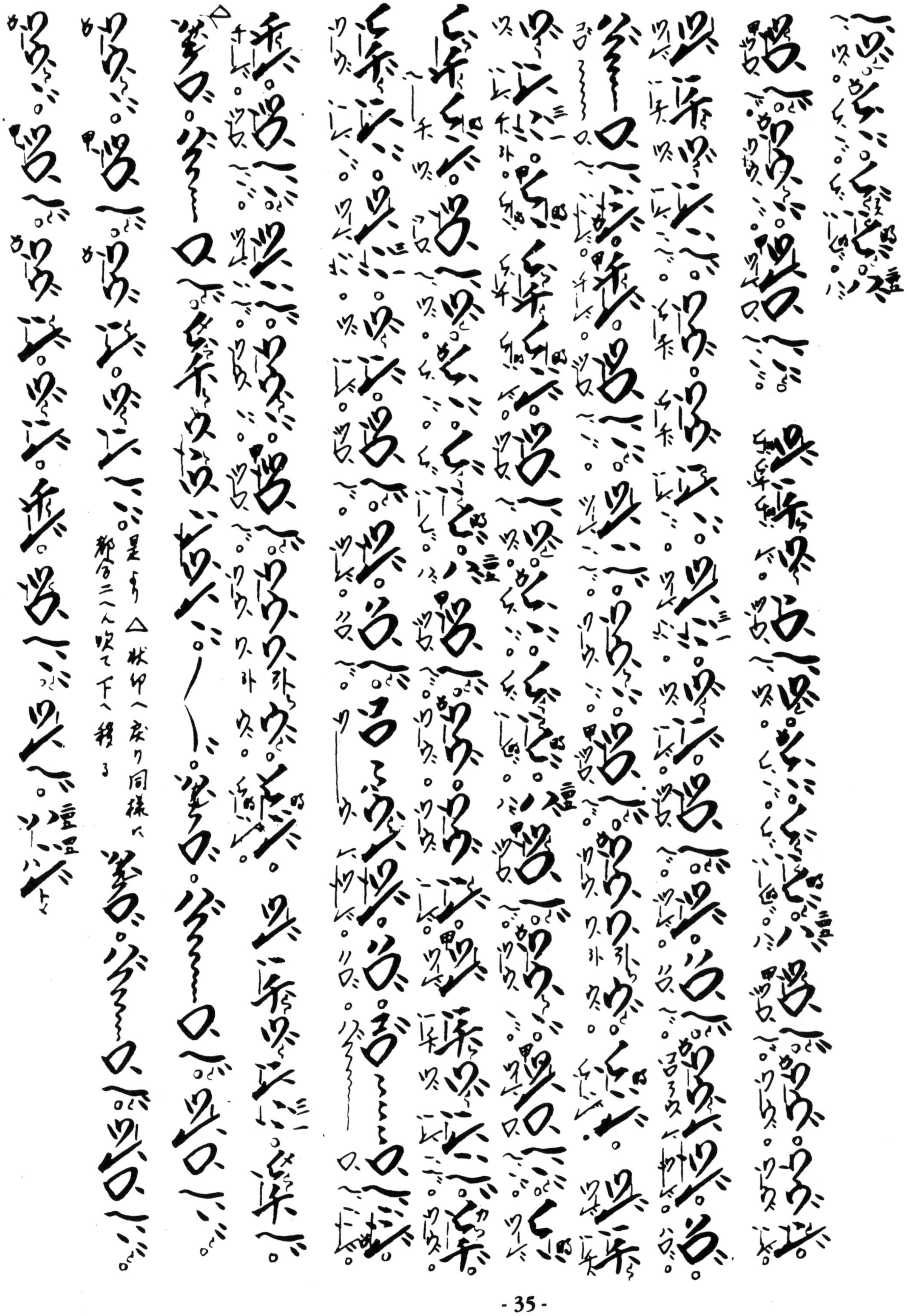
是より△状印へ戻り同様ハ
都合二へん吹て下へ移る

吟龍霊空

下野虚霊

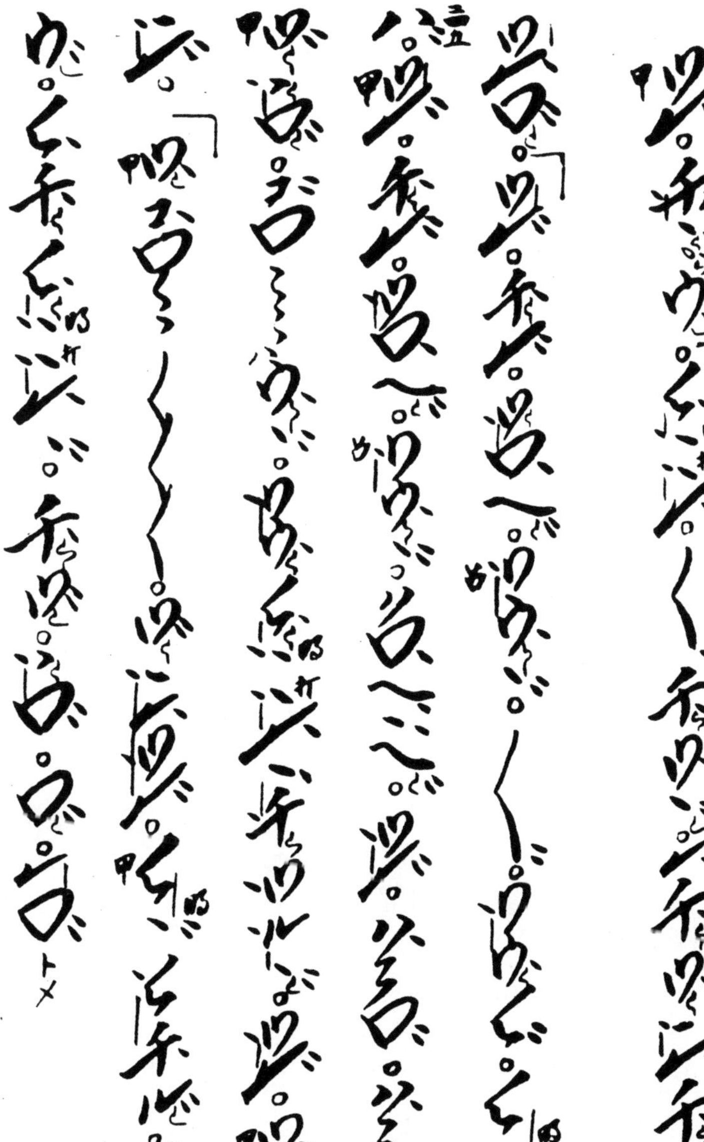

厂音桂の曲

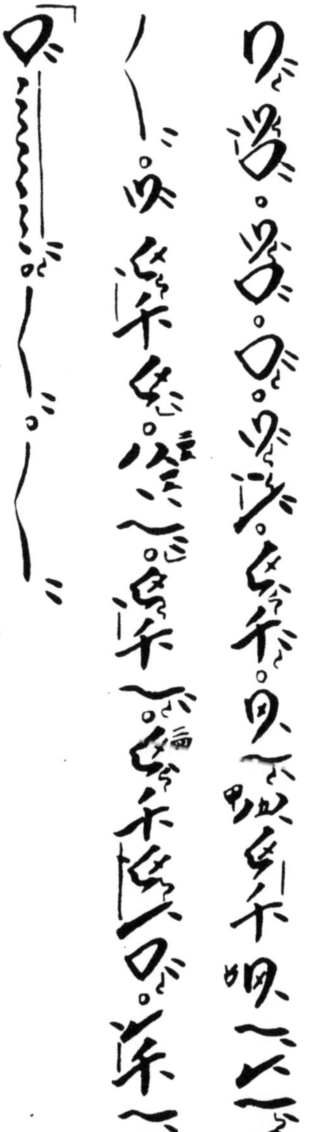

芦(アシ)の調

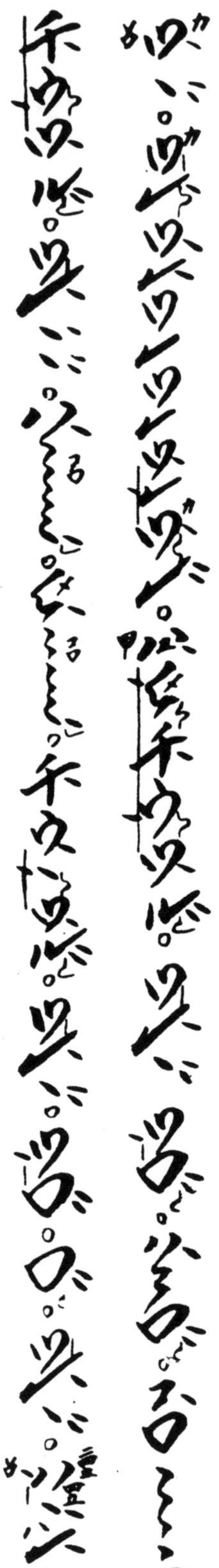

三谷菅垣

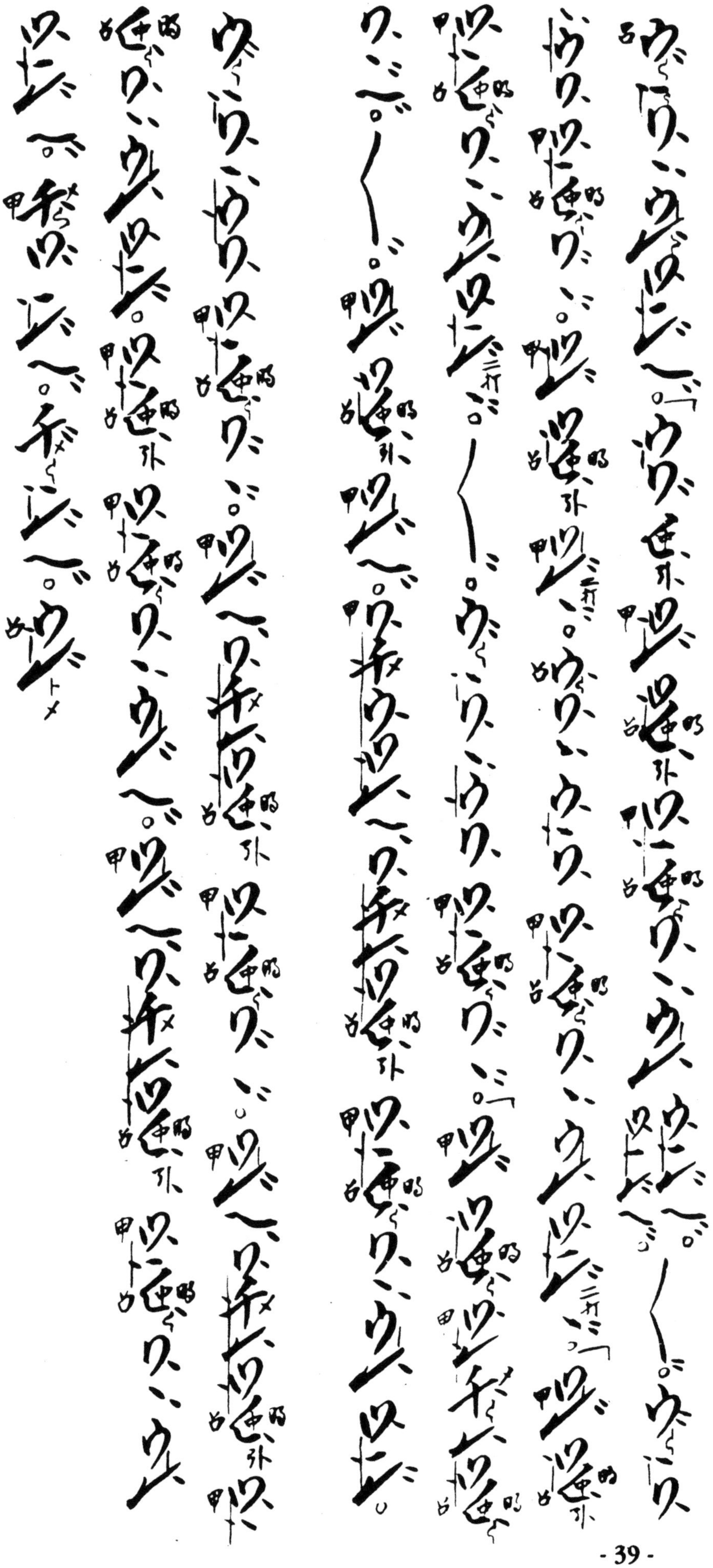

鳳将雛

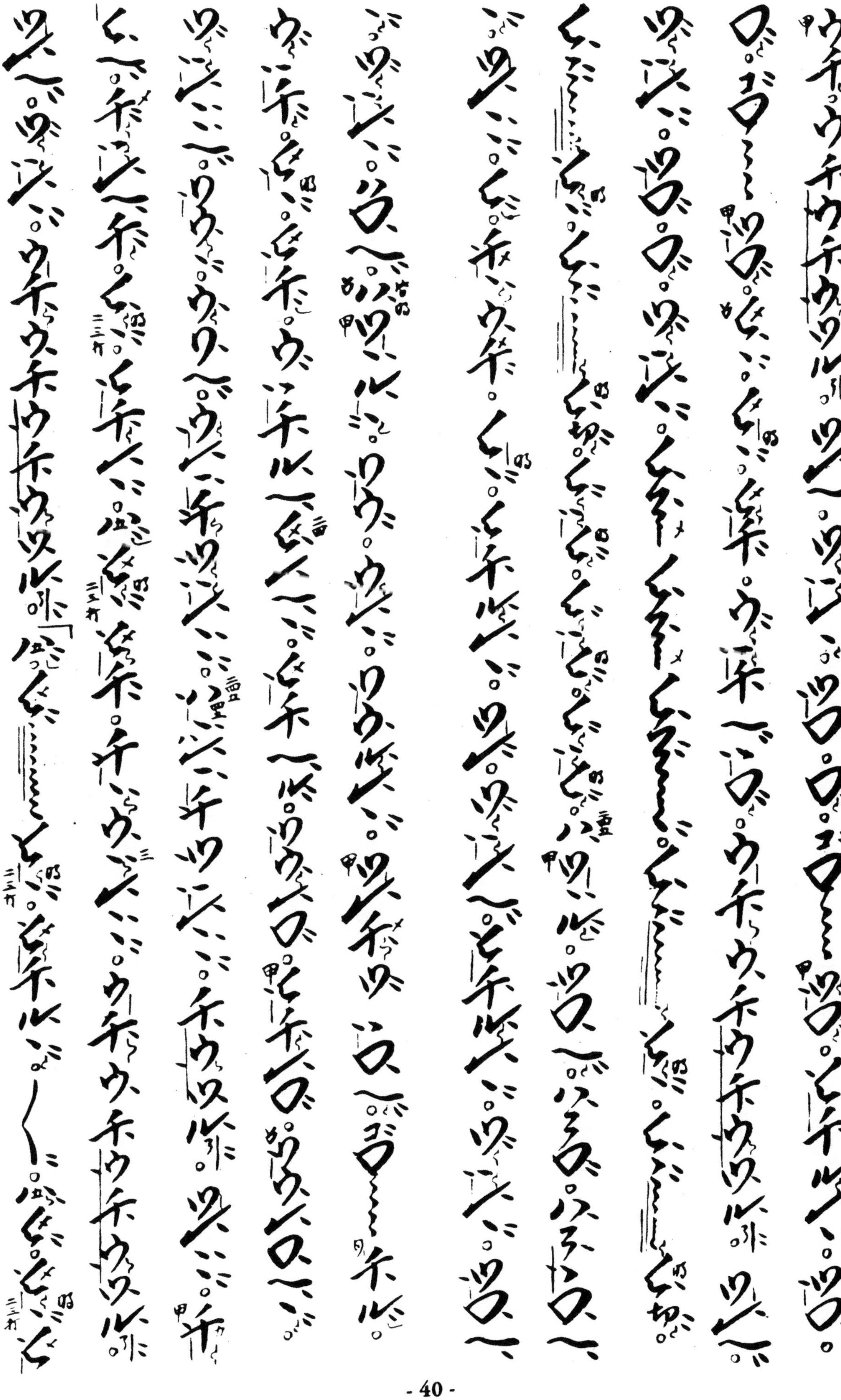

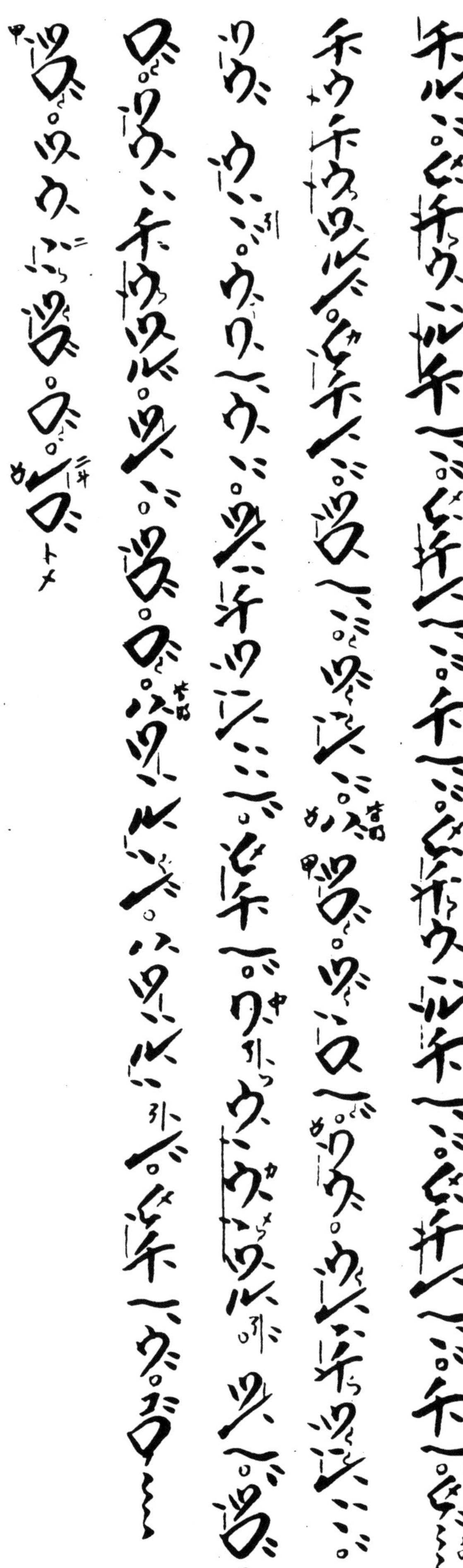

曙調

一二三鉢返曲、一尺八寸にて吹く時
此曲一尺三寸にて合ふ

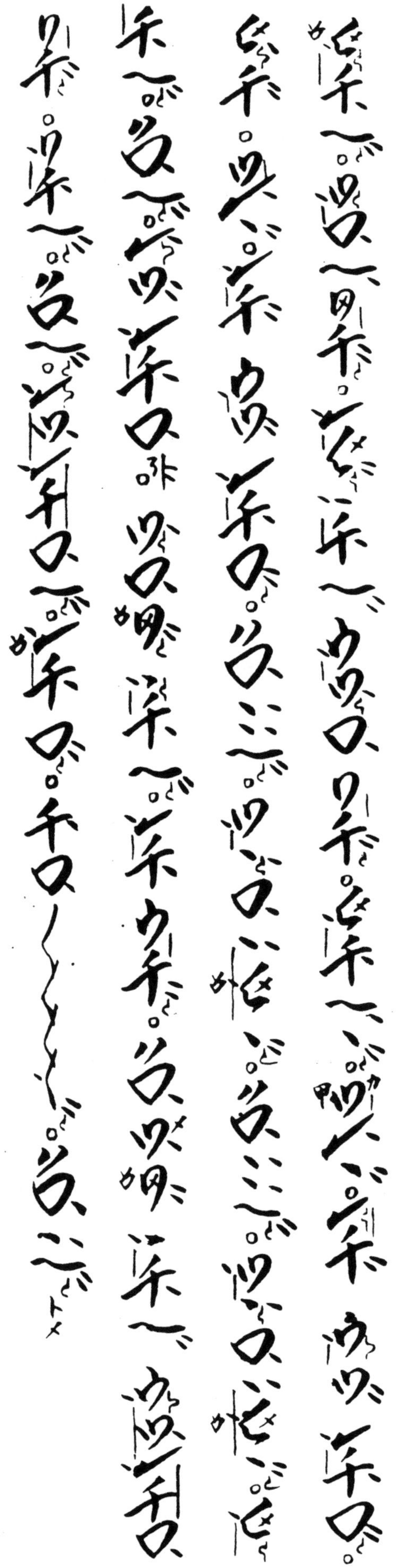

曙菅垣

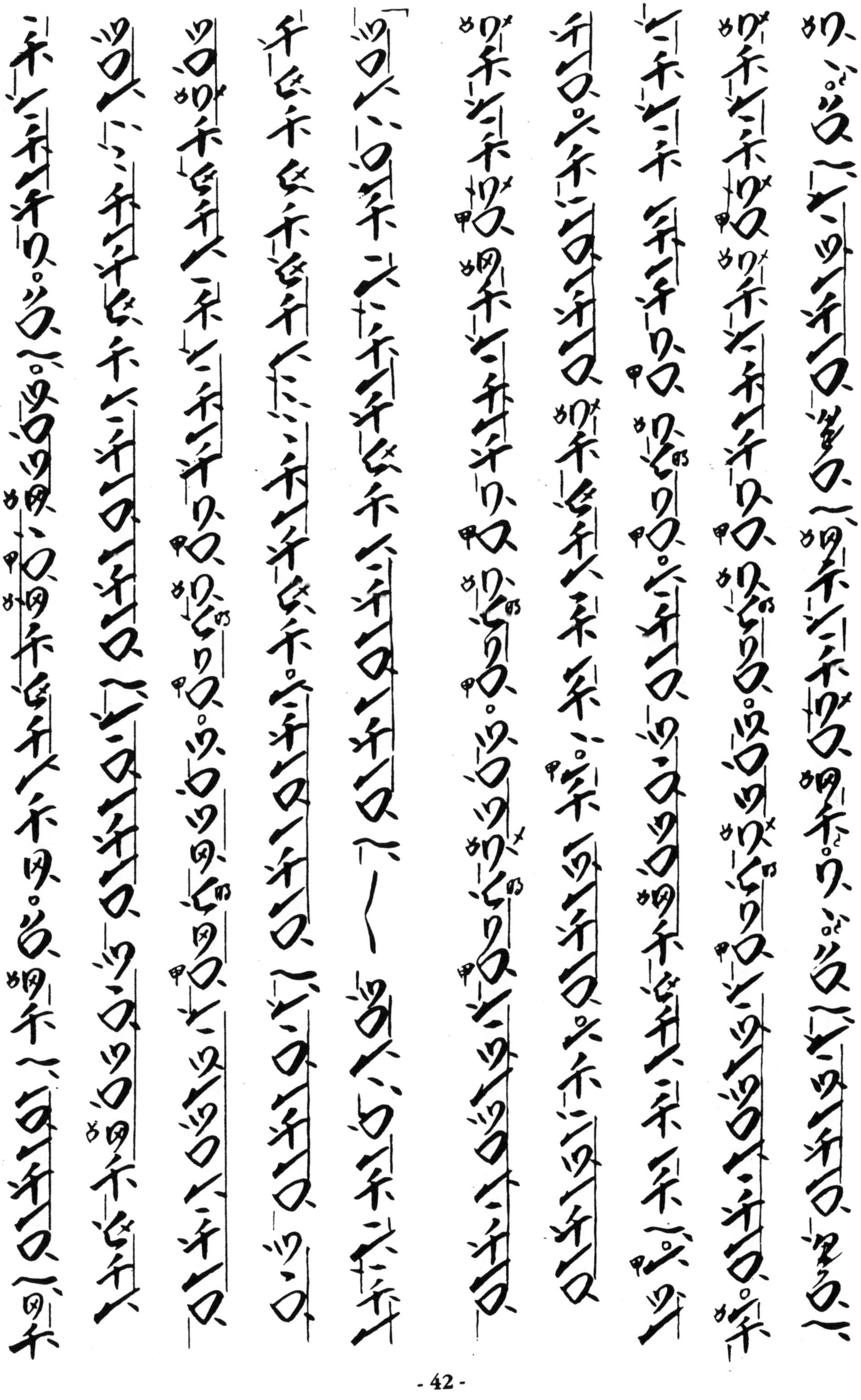

波間鈴慕

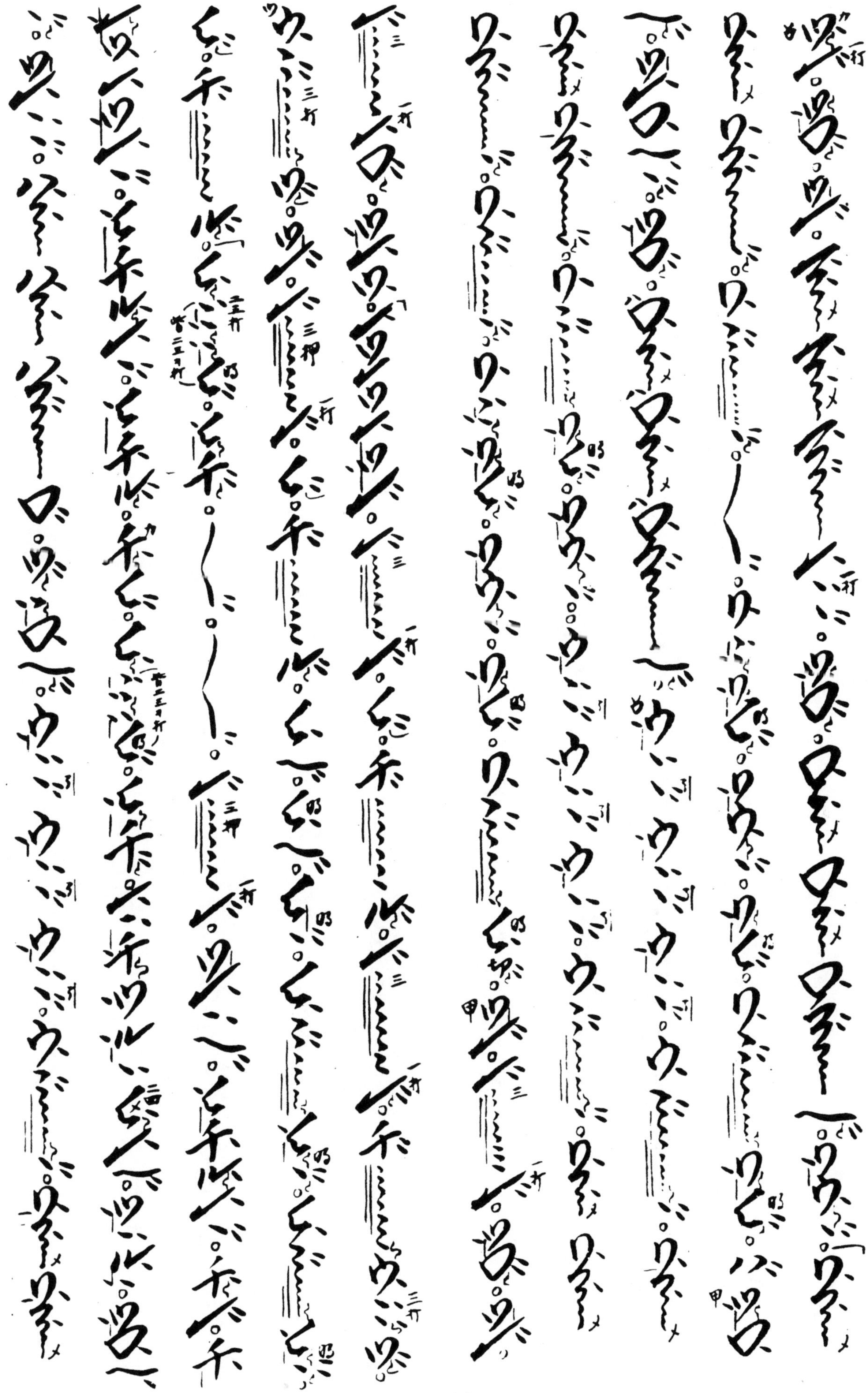

毬と殿様

紅屋の娘

花嫁人形

雨降りお月さん

(rest)

NOTE: The MERI of a note is often indicated by a slash through the note instead of a symbol next to the note. (乙) is the low octave symbol used in this notation.

「出船

船

お江戸日本橋

黒田節

元禄花見踊

-48-

浜辺の唄

浜千鳥

深川節

靴が鳴る

港

天然の美

茶摘み

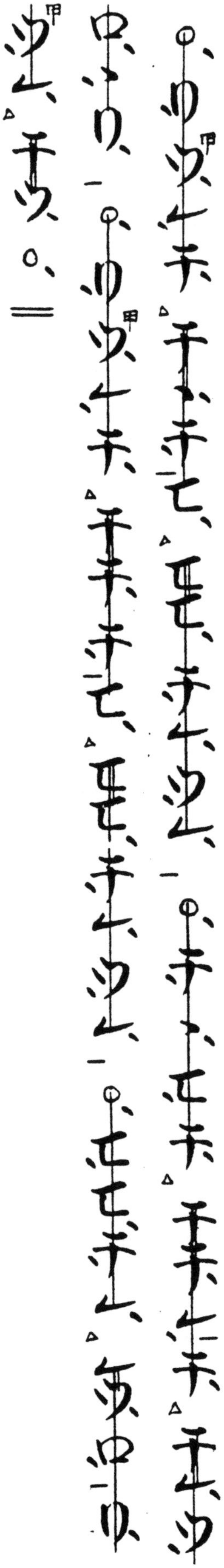

かっぽれ

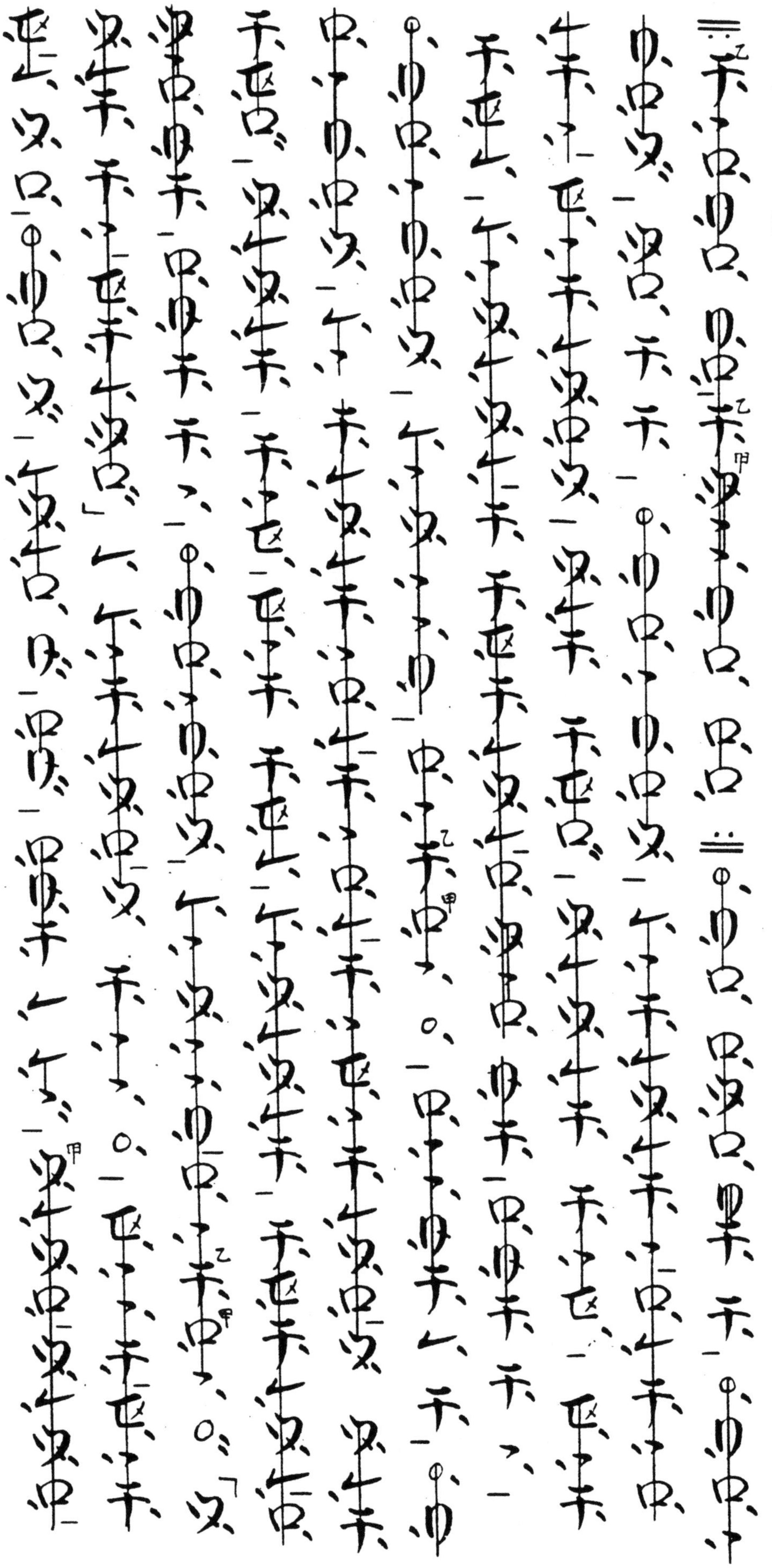

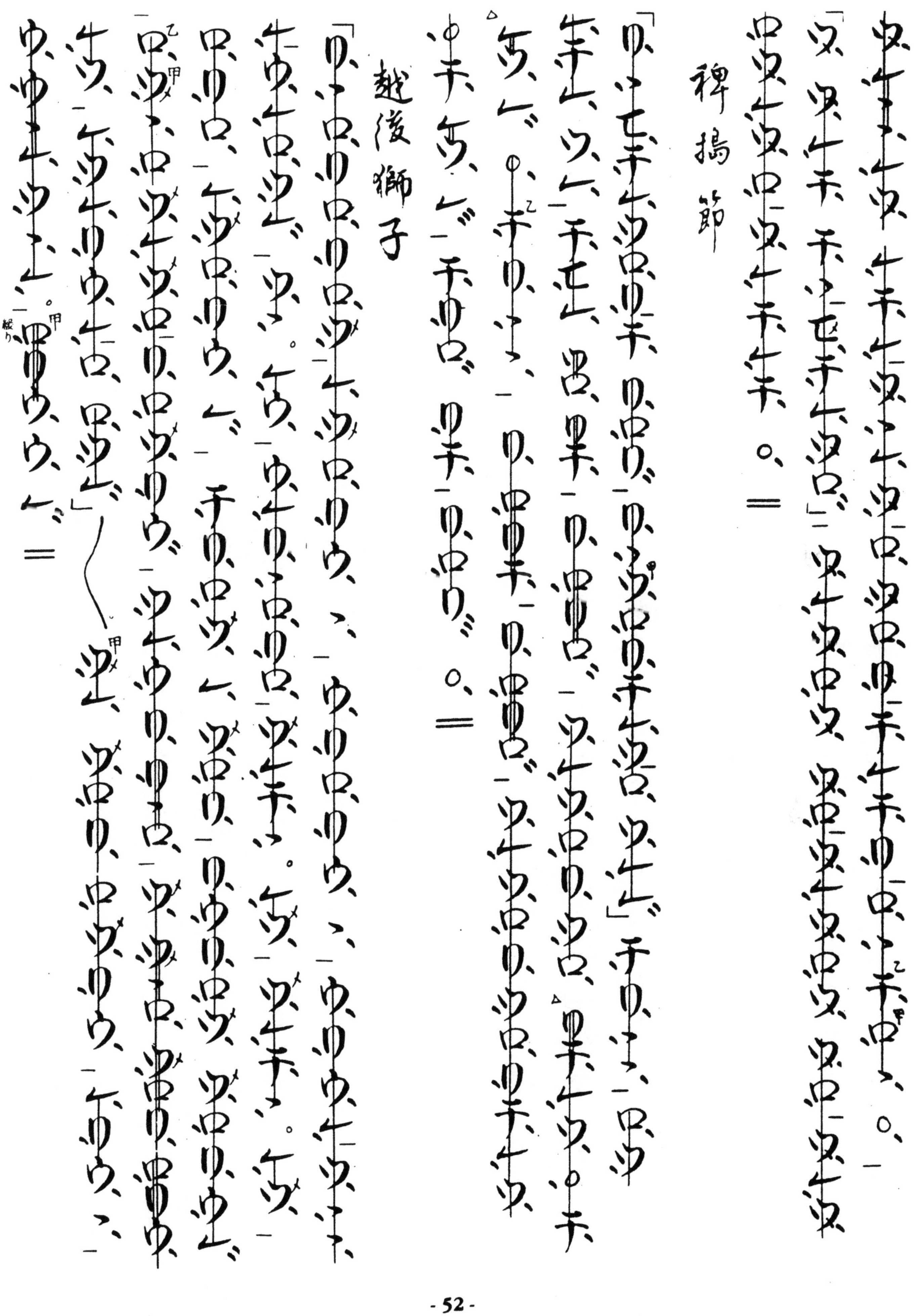

稗搗節
越後獅子

春雨

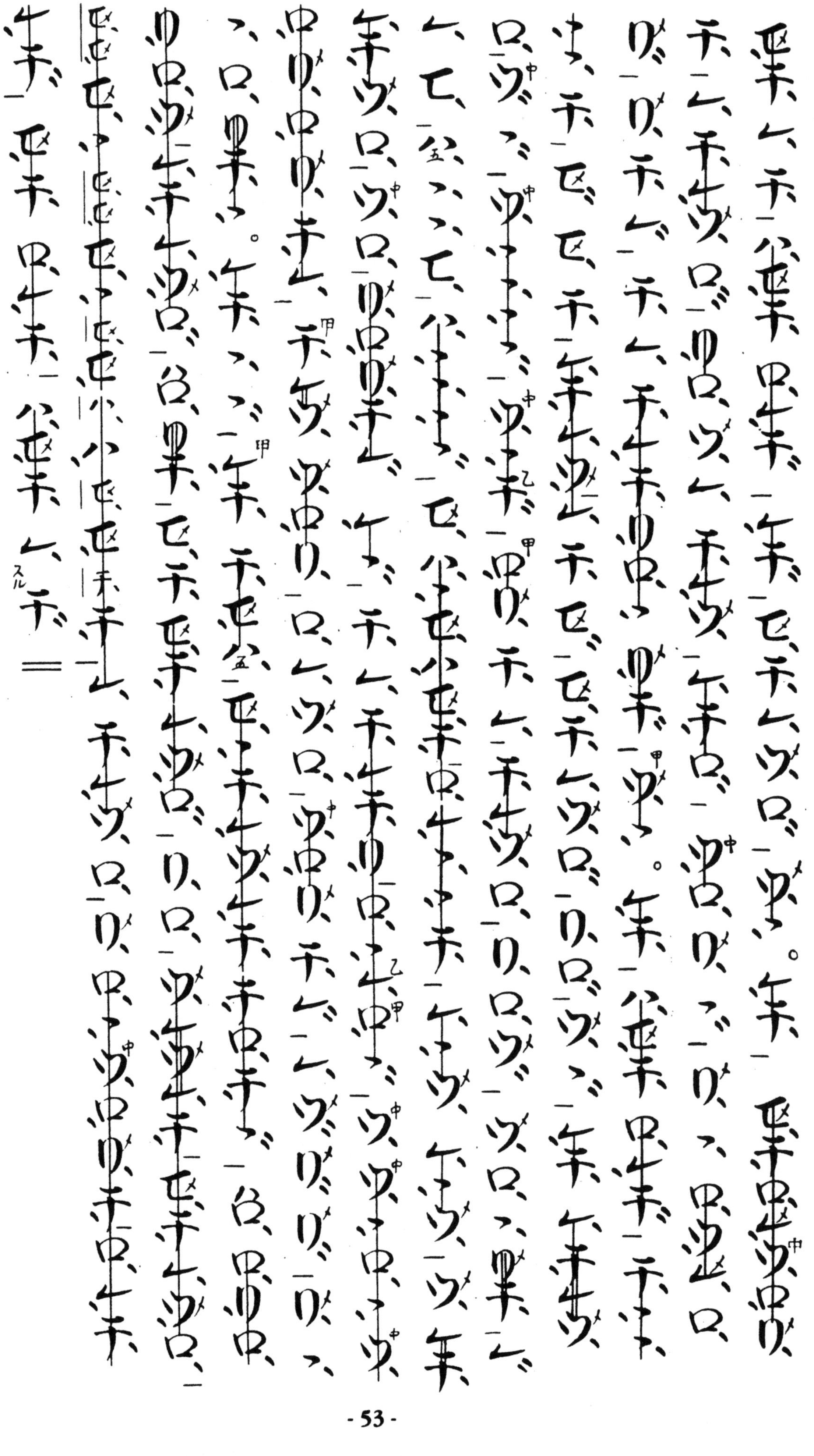

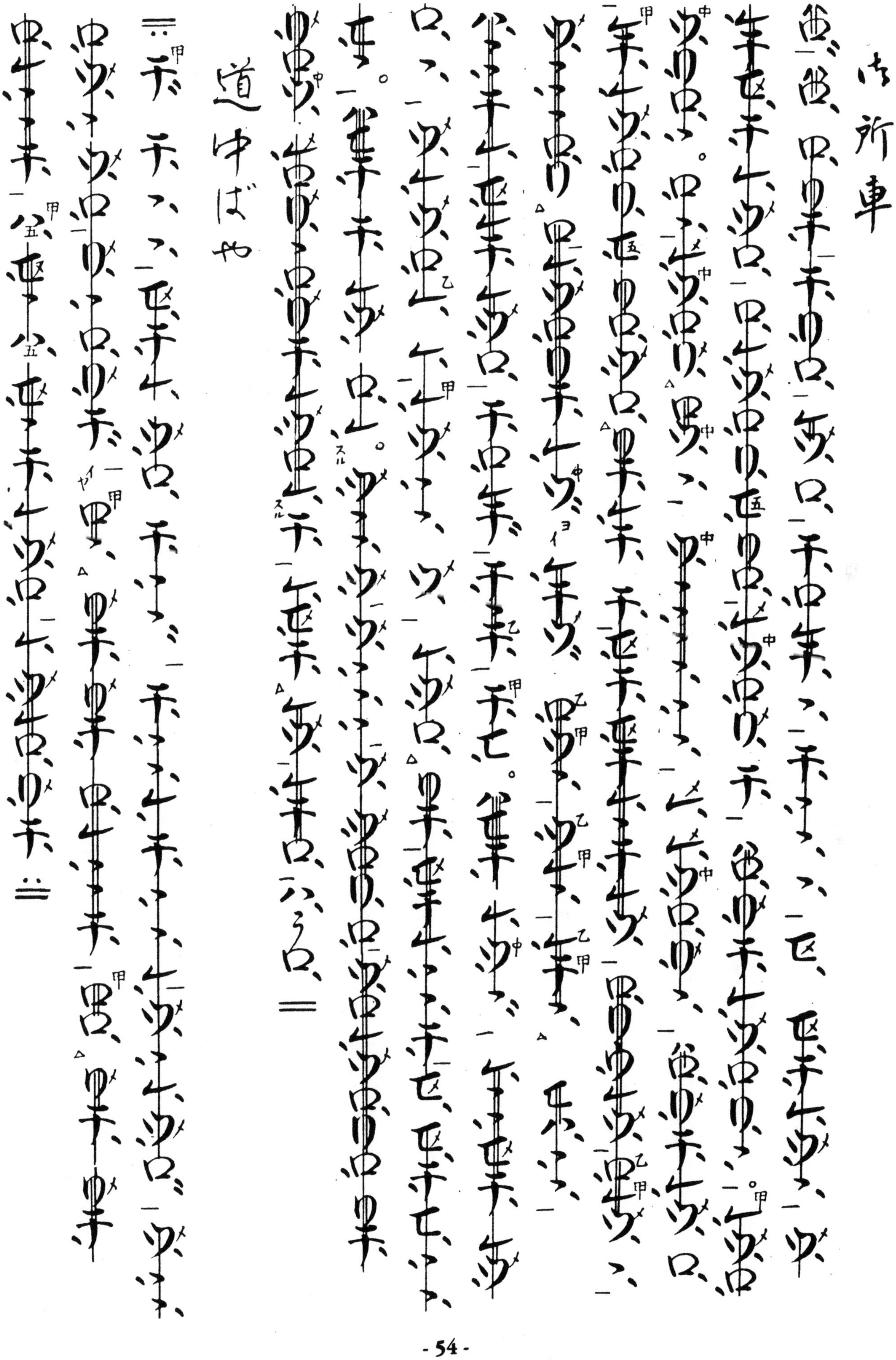
御所車
道中ばや